HELP! I'VE STARTED A BUSINESS

Your guide to running a successful business

Steve Ash

CommsBreakdown

CONTENTS

INTRODUCTION

Starting your own business is a BIG move! It could be the start of a brand-new chapter in your life and an opportunity to do something you're always dreamed about.

A business is a lasting legacy. You can provide employment for your community and bring innovation to your chosen industry. You can build a team of like-minded people, with a mission, a set of shared values and a drive to achieve your company's chosen goals.

It's also a chance to provide a new lifestyle for you and those close to you. If you can build a successful business, that sets the foundations for turning a good profit, boosting your income and providing the kind of home, lifestyle and way of life you've set your heart on.

Let's not sugar-coat it, there's going to be plenty of hard work and tears along the way. But that's outweighed by the potential opportunities you can grab, the achievements you can attain and the difference you can make to the world around you.

Building your business on solid foundations

To build this business right, you're going to need the very best advice. That means getting some pointers on how to set down the foundations of a good business. Ideas on what to include in your planning and how to avoid the common pitfalls. And a raised awareness of some of the complicated (and downright frustrating) areas of being a business owner.

That's where this book comes in. *Help! I've Started A Business* is your 101 guide to becoming a better startup founder and owner-manager. In short, easy-to-read chapters, you get the lowdown on the whole business journey, from start to finish.

You'll find out how to:

1. Define your key idea and build the most comprehensive business plan for the future of the company

2. Get your startup off the ground and start making sales from your new customers

3. Stabilise your finances and get in control of your money, funding and cashflow

4. Grow the business and scale up your operations to meet your long-term goals

5. Meet your aims for the business and decide on your exit strategy.

You can read the book from beginning to end. Or you can dip into each chapter as a self-contained section, as and when you need more help at this stage of the journey. The choice is yours. Unlike some business books, this guide isn't crammed with platitudes and aspirational ideas that could be difficult to put into action. This is practical, straightforward advice for the new entrepreneur. If you're champing at the bit to get started, and want some ground rules to keep you on track, this is the book for you.

Read, digest and learn. But, most of all, follow your heart and aim for the stars. This is your business and its future lies in your hands. Good luck!

◆◆◆

PART 1 – GETTING YOUR BUSINESS IDEA OFF THE GROUND

CHAPTER 1. DEFINING YOUR BUSINESS IDEA

Having that Eureka moment when you cook up a great new business idea is a great experience. You'll be full of ambition and eager to begin building your startup. But once you've had that initial rough idea, how do you assess and plan out your business idea to make sure that it has legs?

For a startup, the key thing is to define what your idea brings to the marketplace. This way, you know WHY you're starting this venture and – crucially – whether it's a viable business model.

Research the existing market and do your homework

A first vital step is to clarify the business purpose of your idea. What does it do, how does it cater to an existing or future need in the marketplace and who will your customers be?

Think about what your product or service delivers to the end customer, and why this customer should part with their hard-earned cash to purchase your offering. Design your product/ service so that it caters to a customer need that you've identified, and make sure your business offers the best solution to that need. In a crowded marketplace, you'll need to stand out.

Check out the competition

Once you know the aim of the new business, it's sensible to start researching your competitors in this space so you can see how your idea compares.

If you're bringing a brand-new innovation to market, you may well be the first entrant in this space. But for most business ideas, there's likely to be another competitor out there – and they'll be eager to take your market share. Research your closest competitors and look closely at their products, services, prices, and their approach to marketing and customer service.

Do the numbers add up?

Getting a great understanding of your financial model is critical to your success. Ultimately, if your idea can't generate revenue, cashflow and profit, it won't sustain a real-world business.

A good starting point is to work out your initial costs. Add up your estimated costs for producing your new product, or delivering your service. Include all your raw materials, your overheads, your labour costs and your delivery expenses etc. Then think about the margin (profit) you need to make per unit, and the price you'll charge to the customer. If you can make enough sales at the right profit margin, will you break even? And will you make a profit?

Write a rough business plan

Every startup needs a business plan behind it. This will be the route map that defines your journey, sets out the key targets and drives the course of the first year or two of the company.

Important items to include in your plan include:

- An outline of your product/service and what it aims to do

- A definition of your key customer and how you'll meet their needs

- An overview of the market – including a SWOT analysis (Strengths, Weaknesses, Opportunities and Threats)

- A summary of your sales, marketing and business operations

- Your key objectives for the first year – and how you'll achieve them

- Your predicted financial return – and how you'll generate these profits

- A breakdown of the initial funding you'll require

- Timescales for each element – so you can track your progress

As the old saying goes, 'Fail to plan, plan to fail'. So, putting time and effort into a well-thought-out business plan could well be the answer to your future prosperity.

◆◆◆

CHAPTER 2. WRITING A MISSION STATEMENT

You've had your initial business idea and written a plan. But do you know WHY you're creating this new business, or HOW you'll deliver your end product/service? What will the company's underlying purpose be and how will your core values drive the business?

To get these crucial elements ironed out, it's a good idea to write a 'mission statement' for your startup – a short summary of the aims and values of your brand-new business.

WHAT does your business do?

The first thing to pin down is what the business actually does – i.e. at the most basic level, what is the output of your new business idea, and what is its purpose.

Defining this 'WHAT' element might sound simple, but describing it in a clear and concise way will help you to begin the process of completing your mission statement. A bicycle manufacturer might define their WHAT as 'making quality bikes at great prices, for adults and kids to enjoy'. Whereas a creative agency might define their WHAT as 'delivering creative solutions to our business clients' design problems'.

HOW does your company do what it does?

Next, have a think about HOW you achieve what you do. How do you deliver your product or service to customers, what operations are involved and what makes your way different?

The bicycle manufacturer might have a big focus on making hand-made bikes, so their HOW could be 'We make our bikes by hand, and to order, using our 25 years' experience in the industry to deliver the best possible quality'. While the creative agency might say 'We use the latest design approaches, coupled with cutting-edge design software, to bring our clients' design to life'. Both of these statements explain the underlying operational processes in the business, and how each business delivers its product/service to the end customer.

WHY does your company do what it does?

Most businesses are great at defining the WHAT and HOW elements of their business model. 'I make Product A using Process B'. But it can be a lot harder to define WHY you're doing this.

Ultimately, the WHY is the most important element of your mission statement. In essence, you're describing what drives you to do what you do. What are your big aspirations for the business, and what do you want to achieve? For the bicycle manufacturer, the WHY statement may be 'We want to encourage our community to get on their bikes, become more sustainable and stay healthy'. And the agency may define their WHY as 'We want to build innovation into everything we do, bringing fresh ideas to our clients' design'.

What are the core values driving your enterprise?

Your personal values as a founder might not sound like a crucial element to think about. But any new startup is a reflection of the ideas, ambition, drive and values of its founders.

The way you behave, the vision you provide for your team and the ways you interact with your first customers will all underline the foundational values of your new business. Think about what drives you. Is it profit and money? Or do you want to change the world in positive ways? Or provide employment and opportunities for your local community?

Bring it all together into your mission statement

If you've answered those four questions, then you have everything you need to create a comprehensive and useful mission statement for the business.

For example, for the bicycle manufacturer, it may look like this:

Happy Spokes Bicycles Ltd:

- **What we do:** We make quality, sustainable bikes at great prices, building a range of city bikes for adults and kids aged 9 to 90 to enjoy.

- **How we do it:** We make our bikes by hand, and to order, using sustainable processes and our 25 years' experience in the industry to deliver the best possible quality.

- **Why we do it:** We believe that cycling is the future. We want to encourage our community to get on their bikes, become more sustainable and stay healthy.

- **Our core values:** Our 5 core value pillars are:
  - **Sustainability** – we strive to limit our impact on the planet and environment
  - **Health** – we aim to make our customers healthier and fitter
  - **Craftsmanship** – we believe in keeping hand-made production alive and well
  - **Value** – we want our bikes to be affordable to all
  - **Fun** – we aim to make Happy Spokes a fun community to be part of.

With your mission statement written, and a business plan under your belt, you have the best possible foundations on which to build your new business enterprise.

◆◆◆

CHAPTER 3.
OUTLINING YOUR
IDEAL CUSTOMER

Customers form the beating heart of your startup. Without a stable customer base, you can't generate sales, bring in income or create a viable business model. So, it's vital for your new business to have a very clear and fleshed-out idea of your 'ideal customer'.

Your perfect customer may well evolve and change over the life of the business, but it's important to define your initial customer audience right from the outset.

Who is the end customer for your products and/or services?

Whenever you create a new product or service, you should have a very specific idea of who your target customer will be. Understanding that customer profile is incredibly important.

Is your ideal customer a high-street consumer, or a procurement manager in a business? Will your audience be younger or older, at the top end of the economic spectrum, or someone with limited cash to spend? Think about the full demographic breakdown of this perfect customer and make as detailed an outline as possible, so you know exactly who you're targeting.

What are the key needs of this demographic?

A good business model provides a solution to a given customer need. Understanding that need in forensic detail is what gives you the power to customise and tailor your offering.

Put yourself in your ideal customer's shoes and imagine their daily lives:

- What are the challenges they face?
- What are the problems holding them back?
- What are their dreams and aspirations?
- What kinds of people do they want to become?

The more information you can glean on their everyday requirements, the more primed you'll be to target those self-same needs.

How does your product/ service meet these needs?

Knowing your customers' key needs is only half of the conundrum. What you have to do now is offer a product or service that actually MEETS these needs, at a price the customer will pay.

Ask yourself, 'what does the customer want, and how can we provide it?'. If you can design the right solution, you're already halfway to creating a new customer. For example, eating enough fresh fruit and vegetables is something we all struggle with. Why not create a food startup that delivers fresh fruit & veg smoothies to people's home or work addresses, making it easier to eat a healthy diet? The 'needs' there are healthy eating, convenience and price. Get it right, and you've filled that customer niche.

How do you intend to reach
this customer audience?

To sell your products, customers must be aware of your brand. So, an important part of your customer research will be understanding which marketing and promotional channels to use.

Knowing where your customers hang out – both online and in the real world – is a critical piece of information when it comes to promotion. In the digital age, there's a baffling mix of different online channels and social media platforms to navigate. But by doing your research carefully, you soon start working out whether your target audience are Facebook fans, or Twitter lovers. The more detailed you can be about these customer preferences, the better you'll get at choosing the right promotional and marketing routes.

Bringing it all together into
a customer profile

By combining all the information you've gathered into one concise customer profile, you give your sales and marketing team a very clear picture of who to target.

This would be the customer profile in our food delivery example:

- **Customer profile:** busy, time-poor professionals in the 25-45 age bracket, with an interest in healthy eating and nutrition

- **Customer need:** finding the time to eat their 5-a-day fresh fruit and veg

- **Our solution:** Fresh fruit & veg smoothies delivered to their home or work address

- **Marketing channels:** train station advertising, Instagram adverts and ads in city gyms

◆◆◆

CHAPTER 4. GETTING FUNDING FOR YOUR STARTUP

A great business idea is an excellent starting point for a company. But without funding to provide the necessary capital, your business idea could be dead before it's even begun.

To quote a well-worn phrase, 'Cash is King' and that means it's critical to start thinking about funding as early as possible in the journey. Think about how much investment you'll need to get going, the different routes to funding and the best ways to approach investors and lenders.

Calculate your startup costs

Working out your startup costs gives you an approximate figure for your initial investment in the business. Armed with this figure, you can start looking at how much cash will be needed to kickstart your initial business idea.

Think about costs like; buying computer equipment, office furniture and desks, equipment and tools, vehicles and all the other things needed to become operational.

Estimate your average monthly expenditure and revenues

In the most basic terms, your startup's financial model is a process of money going out on costs (expenditure) and income coming in from sales and other sources (revenue). Estimating your expenditure and revenue will help you understand if the business can actually generate a profit.

Make a list of your expected monthly expenditure. This could include your office rent, business rates, software subscriptions, the costs of raw materials, your utility bills, staff payroll and any wage you plan to pay yourself. Then, estimate the number of sales you're likely to make in a month and work out the revenue this will generate. For the business to be viable, your revenue MUST be larger than your expenditure. If not, you'll never have any profits at month-end.

Review your funding position

You should now have a fairly good idea of your initial startup costs and your monthly expenditure. It's sensible to give yourself at least 6 months before you start generating meaningful sales revenue, so you'll need to factor this into your funding plans.

If your startup costs come to $5,000 and your monthly costs come to $4,000, you'll need $29,000 up front to kickstart the business ($4k x 6 + $5k). That's a significant amount of money and, unless you're very fortunate, it's unlikely you'll have this kind of cash just sitting around.

So, what can you do to raise this funding?

Explore different routes to funding

There are plenty of different ways to raise the necessary startup funds. What works best for you and your business will differ depending on your situation, your credit rating and your ability to convince lenders and investors of the viability of your business idea.

Usually speaking, you have the options of:

- Borrowing money from friends and family who believe in your idea

- Borrowing from banks and other lenders who can see the startup's potential

- Appealing to external investors, such a private investors or venture capitalists

- Crowdfunding your funding through sites like Kickstarter or GoFundMe

To make your funding search successful:

- **Know what you need to borrow and why** – be clear about your key objective, why you need to source additional money and how this funding will be used

- **Have a clear budget and financials** – lenders will take you more seriously if you've estimated your budget and have done your homework when looking at the numbers.

- **Look for the best terms and interest rates** – when taking out a loan, shop around and look for lenders who can give you the best possible deal. A loan on unfavourable terms will be more of a hindrance than a benefit.

- **Partner with investors who share your vision** – taking cash from external investors helps to quickly boost your cash reserves, but these investors also need to share your aims and vision for the business. Disagreements can be highly disruptive.

◆◆◆

CHAPTER 5. SETTING UP THE COMPLIANCE FOUNDATIONS FOR YOUR STARTUP

To trade as a business, you need to meet the right compliance requirements. It's certainly not the most exciting part of creating a startup, but setting up the right legal, accounting and tax compliance foundations ensures that you're doing everything by the letter of the law.

Here are the main compliance steps to think about, and why they're so important to the smooth running of your business.

Decide on a legal structure for the business

First off, you'll need to make a decision about the legal structure of the company. There are two key choices here – incorporated (a limited company) or unincorporated (usually either a sole trader or a partnership). The key difference here is around liability. In other words, do you want your business to be a limited company, where you and the business are treated as separate legal entities? Or do you want to be unincorporated, like a sole trader, where you and your business are seen as one single entity.

Most startups will opt for the incorporated limited company route, keeping your personal and business finances separate and lowering your personal liability and risk.

Open a business bank account

To trade, take payments and pay your suppliers, you need to have a business bank account that's separate from your own current account. This helps to create a tangible divide between the money you've generated from the business, and your own personal cash.

Most high-street banks won't let you use a personal current account for business purposes. Banks will offer a variety of different business accounts, with varying levels of fees, overdraft levels and additional business features. Set up the business account and then use this account for ALL transactions going in or out of the company.

Set up a bookkeeping and accounting system

It's a legal requirement for your limited company to keep adequate records and to submit annual statutory accounts. To be able to meet these requirements, it's essential that you have a bookkeeping process and a reliable accounting system in place.

There's a dazzling choice of different cloud-based accounting platforms aimed at the ambitious startup owner. Xero, QuickBooks, MYOB and Sage are big names in this space, and all offer easy-to-use systems that make the accounting process relatively straightforward. It's a good idea to engage an accountant, right from the start, to get the best possible accounting advice.

Register for the relevant business taxes

Tax is an unavoidable part of running any business. It's mandatory for you to register for the relevant business taxes, and you'll also need to factor in that a certain percentage of your startup's profits will end up going to the tax authorities at the end of each financial year.

If you've opted for the limited company route, you must register for corporation tax in your home territory. Corporation tax is paid based on a percentage of your year-end profits, once reliefs and other allowances have been taken into account. The rates change from country to country, but the current worldwide average is 25.44%. That means that a quarter of your end profits will end up being paid over in tax, so it's imperative that you put this money away in a separate tax account, or ring-fence it in your accounts, so you have the money to pay the bill at year-end.

Other taxes to register for include:

- **Self-assessment income tax** – although you'll pay corporation tax on your company's profits, directors are also taxed on their own personal earnings too. If you're an unincorporated sole trader, this is also the way you'll be taxed on your business profits, as your personal and business income are treated as the same thing.

- **Goods & Services Tax (GST)** – GST (or Value Added Tax [VAT] in the UK and Europe) is an indirect value-added tax or consumption tax for goods and services. If you sell products or services that qualify for GST/VAT, you're responsible for collecting these taxes and paying them to the tax authority on a monthly, quarterly or annual basis.

- **Pay-as-you-earn (PAYE)/Pay-as-you-go (PAYG)** – if you have employees, and your home territory operates a PAYE/PAYG system, you'll need to make income tax deductions from your employees' wages and pay these taxes directly to the relevant tax authority. This is all done via your regular payroll run.

◆◆◆

CHAPTER 6. HIRING EMPLOYEES FOR YOUR STARTUP

When setting up your new venture, the people you hire may well become the most important assets in your business. They're your trusted workforce, the face of your new brand and the people you've entrusted with getting your business idea out into the real world.

Because of this, it's vital that you choose the right talent, the right personalities and the right mix of people for your team. Making a mistake with your hiring at such an early stage can really hold you back, so be sure to put some real thought into who you need on the team.

Consider which roles you need to start operating

Getting your startup to the 'Minimum Viable Product' or MVP stage is a big turning point for the business. From a staffing point of view, you need to think about what roles will be needed to get you to this stage – so you have enough hands on deck to really become operational.

Could you do everything yourself and become a jack-of-all-trades? Or will you need salespeople, marketers, operations managers and shop-floor staff to get this thing going? In an ideal world, you obviously want a big, effective team to kickstart your operations, but payroll costs and your available funding will put a limitation on this. Think about which roles you REALLY need and start off with a skeleton crew (but without the need for a ghost pirate ship!).

Decide whether to outsource or go in-house

Once you have a list of your core roles and skeleton team, you then have another important decision to make – which of these roles will be full-time, in-house employees? And which roles will be part-time, or outsourced to freelancers and contractors?

Having full-time employees on the books gives you a permanent resource, with a team who are wholly focused on bringing your MVP to market. But employees are costly. Aside from monthly wages, you need to pay for holiday pay, sick pay and a staff pension scheme. A more cost-effective option can be to use freelancers at the early stages of the business, hiring in talent and resources as and when you need them.

Search your network for talent

Knowing the roles you need is one thing, but actually FINDING the talent is another. Use your existing business and social networks and put out the word that you're hiring. Word of mouth can be a great way to find people, but make sure that applicants fit the stated criteria.

Writing short, clear job descriptions for each role is a good way to outline the position, attract the best candidates and filter out the weak applicants. Using a recruitment agency or a jobs website helps to spread your net wider and also takes some of the admin workload away. Once you have a shortlist of candidates, it's time to start interviewing.

Check that applicants share your vision and values

A job interview is obviously about more than just running through the skills on a CV. The successful candidate is going to be working very closely with you, so you need to know that they can do the job but also that they're a good fit for the team.

When interviewing an applicant, ask yourself:

- Do they share your vision for the product/service and the future of the company?

- Do they seem driven, with the right kind of can-do attitude?

- Are they engaged by your company values and the WHY behind your business model?

- And, vitally, do you get on with them as a person?

Having the best mix of personalities and talent in a team is so important. Getting the mix right creates a tight, well-focused team. Get it wrong and you're looking at disharmony, a lack of productivity and a team that's not going to deliver the energy and value you need as a founder.

Measure performance and fit

Once you've hired your key talent and formed a team, the challenges don't stop. As you all pull together to get to that all-important MVP stage and beyond, you'll need to have ongoing performance reviews. This includes checking in on how the team is performing as a group, whether there are any teething problems to iron out and how individual employees are tracking against their personal remit, targets and goals.

It's not an easy ride, but with a positive, well-engaged team behind you, you give your new venture the best possible chances of success, growth and long-term prosperity.

◆◆◆

CHAPTER 7. GETTING YOUR OPERATIONS UP AND RUNNING

Once you have the plan, funding and team in place, it's time to think about 'pressing go' on your startup. But what are the key elements to have in place before you begin trading?

The complexity of your operational model will vary greatly, depending on the kind of business you're setting up. A small two-person design agency will have a simpler operational set-up than a wholesale food production business, for obvious reasons. So, this stage of the journey is about pinning down those key operational needs and getting an effective strategy together for how this business is going to work, in the real world.

Find your premises or workspace

Every business needs some kind of workspace, whether it's your own home, an office or a factory space. This is the place where the actual work will be done and the central hub of your operations, so put some careful thought into what space will be needed.

Our two-person design agency could feasibly operate from a coworking office, a startup incubator space or (at a pinch) from a spare room/garage/summer house in the founder's home. The wholesale food production business, however, will need factory space to house its production equipment, a chilled store for the food, an office for the admin staff and managers, and space for delivery vehicles and incoming supplier deliveries etc.

Buy your equipment and tech

You'll have set aside some of your initial funding to buy the basic equipment and technology needed for the business. This will include all the machinery, plant, office furniture, IT, computing and telecommunications equipment required to run the business, plus any vehicles you'll need.

Once you have your premises ready to roll, you can start moving your equipment in and actually 'setting up shop' in your brand-new workspace.

Source your key suppliers

Most businesses will rely on some form of supply chain to keep the business ticking over. The design agency will probably need paper, printer ink and (no doubt) a lot of coffee to stay operational. And our food production business will need raw ingredients, cardboard boxes and product packaging to be able to produce their key products.

Your next step is to source the suppliers you need and set up contracts with these external companies. You may have pre-existing contacts in the industry, or you may be starting with a clean slate. Either way, it's important to build up a trusted supply network, where you've negotiated a good price and decent payment terms. Ultimately, your business can sink or swim based on the stability of your supply chain, so these relationships will be crucial to your success.

Get the logistics and delivery elements in place

Getting the finished product/service to your end customer is the main goal of any business, so the final piece of your operational puzzle will be sorting out your logistics and delivery systems.

For a small service-based startup, like the design agency, the end offering is likely to be either wholly digital or a mix of print and digital. The end delivery process is relatively straightforward and will mostly consist of getting the final signed-off assets to the customer. For a complex manufacturing or production startup, like the food business, the delivery systems will be a vital part of their offering. As a food business, you've got to meet all relevant food hygiene timescales and standards, and get your fresh, high-quality food products safely to your customers.

A delivery system should be customised to each company's specific needs, so it's sensible to put plenty of thought into making this system efficient, cost-effective and productive.

◆◆◆

CHAPTER 8. TAKING OUT THE RIGHT BUSINESS INSURANCE

When you're operating a trading business, it's sensible to think about business insurance.

Whatever kind of business you're running, there's always going to be a certain element of risk. What if a client sues you? What if an employee injures themselves on your premises? What if your workshop catches fire? The list of potential risks is long and, on the whole, it's very difficult to predict when a challenging situation is likely to rear its ugly head.

Because of this inherent risk level, the sensible thing to do is to take out some business insurance. These insurance policies cover you for different eventualities and will mean that you're covered financially if disaster does strike.

But a quick glance at any business insurance website will reveal a wealth of different kinds of insurance to choose from. So, which insurance does your business actually need?

Choosing the right insurance for your sector and business

Business insurance is a complex area to navigate. There are plenty of insurance options to choose from and many of them can be highly specialised. There are, however, certain basic insurance policies that most business owners will need.

So, what are the main insurance types to consider?

Public liability insurance

As a business, you have a duty to keep your customers (and the general public at large) safe while carrying out your operations. If a customer or member of the public is hurt, or their property is damaged by a representative of your business then they may well take legal action to sue you. Public liability insurance covers the legal costs and compensation payments if your business is held responsible for the injury, or for any damage to the person's property.

Employer liability insurance

If one of your employees sustains an injury, or gets sick because of your company's working conditions, they may well make a claim against you. Employer liability insurance protects your business against legal and compensation expenses when an employee makes a claim. If you employ staff, it's compulsory to have an employer liability policy in place (unless you solely employ close family members). This policy is there to safeguard the business, to protect your employees and to cover the significant costs of settling an employee's claim.

Professional indemnity insurance

If you deliver your service or advice to your end customer and they're unhappy with the end result, this can lead to problems. There's always the chance that your disgruntled customer will make a claim for compensation. Professional indemnity insurance protects your business (if you're a limited company) or you (if you're a sole trader or contractor) against a claim from an unhappy client. It will usually cover legal fees and compensation up to a certain amount.

Product liability insurance

This is similar to professional indemnity insurance, but covers you for legal costs and compensation if a customer is injured by a faulty product (rather than a service) that your business has designed, built or supplied.

Commercial property insurance

When you own or lease your own business premises, you'll definitely need to think about insuring your business property.

There are two main types of commercial property insurance:

- Building insurance, and

- Contents insurance.

Building insurance protects your premises against fire, flood, weather damage or other threats to the fabric of the building. It will usually cover the costs of repairs and/or rebuilding. Contents insurance covers your business-related assets that are inside the building. This could be your stock, your office furniture, your computing equipment or any other items covered by the policy.

Home-working insurance

Over the pandemic, far more people have become either permanent or part-time homeworkers. And if your employees are working from their own home, rather than your premises, it's important to check if they're covered by your current insurance. Your employer liability insurance should cover homeworking, but make sure this is specified in the policy. It may also be that your employees are not fully covered by their own home insurance if they're now working permanently from home. It's a good idea to inform their insurance provider and to check whether they need to extend their home insurance policy to cover home-working and remote working.

Travel insurance

We may have seen far less overseas and national travel over the pandemic, but travel is starting to bounce back as the world has opened up again. If you or your employees are going on work-related trips, you should look carefully at getting the right travel insurance for the trip. Your policy should cover illness, medical fees, cover for your business equipment and the costs of any alternative travel arrangements (if your planned flights/trains/transport is cancelled etc.)

Looking for industry specific insurance

By signing up for the main types of business insurance, you can be confident of trading with all the most likely risks covered and accounted for.

It's worth noting that many insurers will also offer tailored, industry specific insurance for different sectors and business types. So, there will be specific insurance policies for freelancers, construction businesses, hospitality companies or creative agencies etc. Talking to an insurer that specialises in your industry is a good way to cover all your bases quickly, with policies that are customised to fit your exact circumstances as a business.

None of us know exactly what lies around the corner when it comes to running a business. So, making sure you're fully insured takes away some of the worry and reduces the main risks.

◆◆◆

CHAPTER 9.
MARKETING AND
PROMOTING YOUR
STARTUP

Even with the best products and/or services in the world, you won't make many sales if your intended customers don't know about your business. To raise awareness of your brand and to kickstart your sales process, you need to start marketing and promoting the company.

Sales and marketing don't have to be complicated, but it is important to have a clear idea of your customers' preferred channels and how you can engage with them in these places.

Create a website and an
online/digital presence

We live in a digital world, so having a presence in the digital space will be vital – somewhere your potential customers can engage with you and begin buying your products.

Start with a website of some sort – a place that will become your digital shopfront and the hub around which your marketing will function. For small micro businesses, this could be as simple as creating a Facebook business page, but most serious small businesses should invest in a full-scale website. Buy a domain name for the company (the companyname.com part) and work with content writers and web designers to create an engaging online site for the business.

Focus on your key messages, tell me (the customer) exactly what you do, and make it as easy as possible to use and navigate the site.

Set up a sales team and start engaging with customers

To push your sales engagement, you need a sales team – or at the very least, one person who's focused full-time on sales and business development.

As a new business, you're entering a market where (at present) most of your target audience are unaware of your products/ services. With a sales team in place, you can start to field enquiries, arrange product demos, book meetings with targets and begin the process of engaging with your chosen customer audience.

People buy from people, as the saying goes. So, building relationships, extending your network and filling your sales funnel will be an essential part of the company's growth.

Make the most of your social media presence

Your website will be your main digital hub, but having a social media presence is also a critical part of building engagement and creating meaningful relationships with your customers.

Facebook, Twitter, Linkedin and Instagram are all good social media platforms to consider. What's important is to research where your target audience hangs out online. For example, if your ideal customers are all on Facebook, there's no point posting much content on Twitter. Choose the most relevant social platforms and use these accounts to post regular content and engage with your audience. Social media is NOT a direct sales channel, but it IS a great place to build customer relationships and promote the values of your brand.

Other ways to raise awareness of your brand

With a website, marketing team, sales team and a solid group of followers on social media, you set some solid foundations for getting your startup's marketing off the ground. But these are just the basics and there's LOTS more you can get involved in to boost your marketing.

For example:

- **Start blogging and using content marketing** – writing a regular blog, or recording video pieces as a vlog, provides your customers with great insights into the business. You could give your opinion on changes in the industry, post news about the company, or share helpful content that adds some meaningful value for your audience.

- **Test out targeted digital advertising** – targeted advertising helps you focus your marketing and advertising on a highly specific audience. You could target customers by their age, their location, their income bracket or their interests – all of which helps you to target your key audience and improve the likelihood of engagement and conversion.

- **Run events and webinars** – events are an excellent way to improve your customer relationships. Having an in-person workshop gets you face to face with your audience, and online options like webinars and live broadcasts help you to raise the profile of your people and begin building online relationships with the right people.

- **Engage with customers through messaging apps** – consumers are increasingly moving to live chat, chatbots and messaging apps as their primary choice when contacting a business. If you can engage well with customers in real-time, via live chats, you can offer a truly personalised way of offering customer support.

- **Expand your profile as a founder** – becoming 'the face' of your new startup is not something that every founder will want to do. But becoming well known within your sector, industry or market is a great way to promote the business as a whole. By sharing thought leadership pieces, appearing on podcasts or becoming a conference speaker, you open yourself up to a wider audience. And when more people know about YOU, more people will also find out about your BUSINESS too.

As your startup grows, your sales and marketing activity will grow too. But getting the basics right at this early stage will get you off to a positive and productive start.

◆◆◆

CHAPTER 10.
MAKING SURE YOUR STARTUP FINANCES ARE IN ORDER

Getting your head around the basics of bookkeeping, accounting and good financial practice may not come naturally to all business owners. But the better you understand the numbers, the more control you'll have over your business and your decision-making.

To get you started, here's a rundown of some of the main financial terms and how they apply to the financial management of your startup.

Revenue and money coming into the business

Revenue is how accountants refer to the income you generate through your sales. If you multiply your average sale price by the number of units sold, this is the top-level number you get. It's a gross figure (i.e. before any deductions) and gives you a clear idea of how much money the business is generating through its sales activity.

Revenue can come from various sources, and each income source is known as a 'revenue stream'. Revenue streams could include product sales, income from services you provide, income from intellectual property you own (like patents) or income from assets the business owns, like property you rent out at a profit.

Having several revenue streams is a good idea. It spreads your income generation across multiple areas and reduces the risk of one revenue stream drying up.

Expenditure and money going out of the business

Expenditure refers to any payments you make (either in cash or credit) against the purchase of goods and/or services. In a nutshell, expenditure is the money that's going OUT of the business. It's important to have a good grip on these costs and to make sure you're not spending any more money than is strictly necessary.

Costs that would fall under expenses include your supplier bills, your payroll expenses, your operational overheads and the costs of any raw materials and goods you buy to keep the business running. The less you pay out in these expenses and overheads, the more of your revenue will end up as profit – as we'll see in the next section.

Profit and loss (P&L)

Your profit and loss statement (usually referred to as your P&L) is an incredibly important financial report to get your head around. The P&L summarises your revenues and expenditure over the course of a period – usually for the month, quarter or year that's just ended. From this P&L report you get a breakdown of the profits and losses the business made during that period.

If you make more in sales revenues than you spend in outgoing expenses, you make a profit (and that's vital to your success). For any business to be financially viable, your financial model MUST be able to generate profit. Without profits, the business can't make money, you can't reinvest back into the company to drive growth, and you (personally) won't get paid anything.

Cashflow statements and positive cashflow

Your cashflow statement is another vital tool in your accounting toolbox. To keep the lights on in the business, you need enough available cash to cover your everyday expenses. Your cashflow statement shows you the cash inflows (money coming into the business from revenues etc.) alongside the cash outflows (payments to suppliers, or operational overheads etc).

For the business to have enough cash in the pot, your cash inflows MUST outweigh your cash outflows. This is called being in a 'positive cashflow position' and it's a level of financial health that every startup should aim for. By tracking inflows and outflows, and projecting them forwards in time to create forecasts, you can make sure there's always available cash in the business.

Improving your understanding of the numbers

It takes time to pick up the financial jargon and accounting terms that will help you understand your accounts. But don't despair: as your startup journey evolves you'll gradually begin to get your head around the important numbers, metrics and reports.

Other important finance terms to understand include

- **Turnover** = the total sales revenue made in a period. It's also sometimes called 'gross revenue', as it's the number prior to any deductions being made.

- **Assets** = the things you own in the business, like equipment, property or cash etc.

- **Liabilities** = the things you owe to other people, like bills, debts and loan repayments.

- **Balance sheet** = a snapshot of your assets and liabilities on a given date.

- **Working capital** = your current assets minus your liabilities. In common usage, it's the capital (money) you have in the business to keep the company operational and trading.

- **Funding** = bringing additional capital into the business, usually in the form of business finance products like loans, or through private investment from outside sources.

- **Credit score** = a rating given to the financial health and risk level of the business. The bigger the score, the lower the risk – and the better your access to funding.

◆◆◆

CHAPTER 11. SETTING KPIS AND MEASURING PERFORMANCE

Once you begin trading, you're faced with a new challenge – successfully managing the course of your brand-new business and making sure it's a profitable enterprise.

It's easier to manage your startup's sales and finances when you have access to the best possible information and data about your performance. Tracking specific metrics and key performance indicators (KPIs) allows you to see how you're performing against your targets – so you can take action to improve performance, sales, growth and profitability.

But which KPIs should you be tracking?

Sales and conversion rates

An obvious metric to track is the number of sales you're making each month. You'll have set a target for these sales in your business plan, so it's important to record each sale and see how the startup is performing over the first six months of the business.

It's also important to log and track the drivers that lead to these sales. How many sales enquiries are you receiving? How many of these enquiries are being converted into actual sales? How many customers are being engaged by your marketing campaigns, and is this engagement leading to interest in your products and/or services.

The more detail you can track from your sales and marketing activity, the more forensic you can get with which campaigns are actually delivering the goods.

Sales revenue and other revenues

When customers buy your goods, that creates income (or revenue) for the business. Ultimately, no business can succeed unless it's generating enough revenue to keep the wheels turning in the business. Because of this, tracking your sales revenue is a vital measure of financial health.

Tracking your various revenue streams over time keeps you in control of your finances and helps you make the right decisions.

With detailed revenue data to analyse, you can:

- Track performance against your revenue targets.

- Forecast how much working capital you'll have at a future point in time.

- Check if there's enough cash in the bank to fund your projects and growth plans.

Cashflow and ongoing cash position

Good cashflow management is all about balancing the process of cash coming INTO the business and cash going OUT of the business. Recording and tracking your cash position is easy to do with the latest cloud accounting software and cashflow apps, so there's no excuse for not tracking your cash position.

Ideally, you want the business to be in a positive cashflow position (with more cash coming in, than going out). But to achieve this, it's helpful to see these cash inflows and outflows in real-time. With up-to-date metrics on your cashflow position, you can make informed decisions about spending, payment of bills and where additional cash and funding may be needed.

Debtor days and aged debt

When customers fail to pay your invoice on time, that creates an aged debt – money that you SHOULD have received but which the customer has yet to pay. An aged debtor report shows you which invoices are unpaid, which customers haven't paid, and the total size of this debt.

Your debtor days number is a metric that shows the average number of days it takes your customers to pay you. Anything above 45 days is bad news, so you want to aim to keep this number between 14 to 30 days, if possible. A large amount of aged debt will leave a hole in your cashflow – and that can quickly start to impact on the day-to-day running of the business.

Gross profit margin

Generating a profit is crucial to the continued success of your startup. Having metrics to measure your profitability is an important part of managing your finances.

One common way to do this is to track your gross profit margin. This metric shows the amount of profit made BEFORE you deduct things like overheads and the cost of goods sold (COGS), shown as a percentage. The formula for calculating your gross profit margin looks like this:

- Gross Profit Margin = Gross Revenue minus COGS, divided by Net Revenue, multiplied by 100

- Deduct your COGS value from your gross revenue to find your gross profit.

- Divide this gross profit by your revenue.

- Multiply the resulting number by 100 to get a percentage.

- This is your gross profit margin as a percentage of gross profit.

- A percentage of 50% to 70% is healthy, but aim for as big a margin as possible

By keeping a close eye on these financial metrics and KPIs, you have the best possible insight into the performance of your new startup – and that's invaluable as your startup journey unfolds.

◆◆◆

CHAPTER 12.
LEARNING TO MAKE
GOOD BUSINESS
DECISIONS

Making good business decisions is easier to do when you have excellent information at your fingertips – and that's the value of having great reporting at the heart of your startup.

Any cloud accounting software worth its salt will offer you straightforward ways to run your financial reports and track your important metrics. That's standard in the new digital world. This level of reporting gives you real, tangible data to base your decision-making on. But good decision-making isn't just about the numbers.

As well as having an effective understanding of your finances, you need a sense of what's good for the business, how decisions will impact on your growth and what your future path looks like.

Run management information
at least once a month

Modern cloud accounting software makes it easier than ever to run detailed, up-to-date reporting on your financial position. With the click of a button, you can run numerous in-depth reports and statements that show your past and future position. Doing this regularly gives you a wealth of financial information to inform your decision-making and strategic thinking.

At each stage in your startup's growth, you'll have to make important decisions about your next step – so, it's important to think about the financial implications of any new projects, the amount of cash in the business and the availability of new sources of funding.

Use metrics and projections to inform your decision-making

Setting up a custom dashboard to monitor the most important metrics and key performance indicators (KPIs) is definitely a good idea. Most accounting apps will let you tailor your dashboard, so you can pick and choose the KPIs that are most relevant to your startup.

Set clear and democratic targets for all of your main KPIs and track them on a weekly basis, so you're monitoring the financial heartbeat of the business. If cashflow is looking poor, look at freeing up some cash, or borrowing money to fill the gap. If sales revenues are dropping, put some renewed vigour into your sales activity, or get a new marketing campaign underway to raise awareness of your most profitable products and services.

Talk to your executive team when scenario-planning

You may be the sole founder of your startup, or you may be part of a bigger team of co-founders. But the reality is that no one person can make all the decisions in a busy startup. To get the best overview of a challenge, or to come up with an effective way to grab a potential opportunity, you need to talk to your team – that's the only way to get an effective consensus.

Talk through the current threats and opportunities and run through as many different potential scenarios as possible. What's the best-case scenario, and how can you achieve it? What's the worst-case scenario, and how do you plan for it, if things don't go according to plan?

Work closely with an experienced external adviser

When you're working in the business 24/7, it's hard to see the business in an objective way. Your judgement on some issues can be overly emotional and clouded by internal or political factors. Working with an experienced accountant, business adviser or business coach brings a fresh perspective on the business – both financially, strategically and emotionally.

Having a trusted external accountant on the team definitely helps you get your numbers straight. But they can also bring their knowledge and experience to bear on your strategic thinking, your decision-making and the impact of the business on your own mental health and wellbeing.

You can open up to them about your worries, share your aspirations for the business and bounce strategic ideas off them – taking some of the pressure off your shoulders.

Track how you're measuring against your goals

To meet your goals and make good business decisions, it's helpful to monitor and track your progress against these targets. If you refer back to your reporting and KPI metrics, you can easily measure your performance over time – and take action if progress is starting to slip.

Areas to keep an eye can include your:

- **Cashflow position** – to ensure you've got enough cash in the business to keep your project moving forward and heading towards the agreed end goal.

- **Sales figures and revenue** – so you can see how you're tracking against your sales targets and if the intended revenue from the project is being achieved.

- **Budgets and expenses** – to check that you're not overspending on your project and that the team is being sensible with costs, expenses and essential overheads.

- **Gross margin percentage** – so you can keep the business profitable and aim to meet your profit targets for the period, or year-end.

- **Growth against targets** – to keep the business performing well and growing at the rate you predicted to meet your growth target for the period.

Making a few bad decisions along the way is all part of the learning process. But by monitoring your performance and talking to the best advisers, it's easier to keep the business on track.

◆◆◆

PART 2 – BUILDING GROWTH AND SCALING UP

CHAPTER 13. SCALING UP YOUR BUSINESS AND WORKFORCE

Scaling up your business isn't about steady growth over time. It's about having a clear strategy for quickly expanding the business to achieve full-scale hypergrowth.

Some startups grow organically, adding customers here and there and gradually expanding over time. Scaling up aims to accelerate this process, pushing your growth to move beyond that slow, organic pace. To achieve this, every element of your business model needs to be reviewed, refined and systemised – building scalability into the company from the ground up.

Systemise your processes and
build scalability into your DNA

Scaling up is a fast-paced, hectic and transformative process for any business. But with the right planning, strategy and funding, the return on your scale-up investment can be significant. Systemisation is the starting point and the driver of your efficiency.

The aim of your systemisation process is to make the business ordered, standardised and efficient. Look at how the business works. Write down every process and operational action. Then see how these processes can be made as lean and effective as possible, and aim to make these operations easily repeatable – so they can scale on demand as the business grows.

If any processes can be automated, automate them. Automation is a key driver of productivity and efficiency, so make use of any tech that could help you get more streamlined.

Remove yourself from the everyday running of the business

This may sound counterproductive, but a big goal of a scale-up strategy is to make yourself redundant from the everyday business. If all the operational elements of the business have to pass through you, as the founder and CEO, then that limits your ability to scale.

Remove yourself from the equation, so the business can grow without your everyday input at the operational level. This allows the business to function without you, leaving you with more time to focus on the high-level strategic work. That's more time for business development. More time working on innovation. More time building relationships with customers and suppliers.

Expand your executive team and workforce

Once you've stepped back from the day-to-day tasks, your CEO role can become far more of a driving force behind the growth of the business. But you can't do this single-handedly. You'll need a close and trusted executive team to work with. Plus, an experienced management team who you can delegate to. And an expanded workforce at all levels of the organisation.

As the startup evolves into a scale-up, the business will become more complex and the workload will increase. To cope with this, and keep the company running like a well-oiled machine, you need a team who are ready for the task and fully on-board with your aims.

Increase your operational infrastructure

Hypergrowth of the business means a greater volume of sales and work. To meet this demand, you urgently need to expand your operational infrastructure. That means looking at the size of your workspace. The amount of tech, equipment and machinery you have. And the ways you deliver your end product/service to your increased customer base.

The key here is to apply a LEAN methodology – keeping everything as simple and basic as possible, while also building in the capacity to deal with this increased volume of work. Get the operational procedures out of your own head and turn them into lean, seamless processes. And invest in the equipment and operational systems needed to cope with your increased output.

Look at investment and access to funding

To bring your scale-up plans to life, you'll need to invest heavily in the future of the business. You're likely to need new assets and equipment. Larger premises or multiple workspaces. More raw materials or stock. And a bigger workforce – which will mean a larger payroll each month.

You may be in the fortunate position of having plenty of spare cash in your reserves. But for most potential scale-ups, there's going to be a need for external funding. This could mean you and your fellow directors putting money into the business. It could mean approaching lenders and business finance providers to take out a loan. Or it could mean looking for private investors to plough money into the business. Whatever the source of this additional funding, having a funding strategy to work from is vital – a funding plan that's aligned with your scale-up plan.

Share your strategic goal and growth plan

For scaling up to be a success, everyone in the company must be on board with the idea. Make your growth aims and key numbers transparent, so the whole team is engaged and motivated by these common goals. And make sure you have a detailed scale-up plan that factors in the challenges of expanding your workforce, resources and operational infrastructure.

Think about:

- WHY you want to scale and what the end goal will be
- HOW you will achieve this – and the timescale
- WHO you need on board to make this work
- WHAT new assets and equipment will be needed
- WHERE the funding will come from to bankroll this plan.

◆◆◆

CHAPTER 14. BUDGETING AND MANAGING CASHFLOW

If you want to stabilise your finances and grow the business, working to strict budgets becomes a necessity. Managing the cashflow twists and turns of a project can be hard work. But it's easier to do when you have an agreed budget and can track your spending and performance.

So, what's the best way to stay in control of the budgets you've set? And how can you manage your cashflow position to make sure there's always enough cash to fund the project?

Understand the costs of each project

Starting a project without fully understanding how much it will cost is a no-no. To keep on top of costs, overheads, staff expenses and general spending, you need at least a ballpark figure for this expenditure. In an ideal world, you'll want to be as precise as possible with these costs.

Run through the project from start to finish and highlight every point where there will be costs to incur. It might be the cost of your raw materials. It may be the cost of buying new equipment.

It could be the payroll costs for the people actively working on the project. Break everything down and come up with a total expense for the project. This is your starting point.

Set your budget and track it over time

Once you know your baseline cost for the project, you and your team should decide on the amount of funds to allocate to the budget. Your baseline cost is a starting point, but don't forget to include extra for specific contingencies. What if the project overruns? What if your raw material costs go sky high? What if you need more people to get the job over the line?

Agree on a clear budget and set up your finance system to track spending against this budget. With a cloud accounting system at the heart of the business, it's easy to create a budget and then record and track your spending over time.

Keep a close eye on budgets and project cashflow

One of the big things to remember is that a budget is not a static thing. You'll obviously aim to stick to your initial costs, but prices and availability will affect the total spend over time. Because of this, it's vital to not just write the budget and then forget about it.

Keep a close eye on your budget performance and the cashflow for each project. Being able to review this performance, in real time, should help you avoid overspending, or running out of cash for the project. And when the cash in the kitty is getting low, you can get proactive and look at ways to top up the budget, or rein in spending in other areas of the project.

Take action to maintain your positive cashflow position

Balancing the cashflow scales on a project isn't easy. But when you spot that there's a potential hole in the budget, the important thing is to do something about it, pronto!

Running any project with your fingers crossed that it will 'all work out in the end' is a recipe for disaster. And with such detailed budget reports and cashflow forecasts available with today's finance apps, there's really no need to be disorganised about your spending.

To keep things in check:

● Set up key metrics for each project, to measure spending,cashflow and progress

● Run worst-case and best-case cashflow scenarios, so you're prepared for anything

● Regularly review your spending and look for areas to make savings

● Take on more funding to plug any cashflow holes as they appear.

◆◆◆

CHAPTER 15. MAKING IT EASIER TO GET PAID

Making sure you get paid on time is incredibly important. The process of making sales and generating revenue lies at the heart of any business model. But you can't manage your cashflow effectively or raise any profits if customers don't actually pay their invoices.

The easier you make it for customers to pay you, the faster you'll see cash coming into the business. That's good news for your financial position, your ability to cover your operational costs and your capacity to fund the growth and expansion of your business.

So, how do you speed up those payments and make sure you get paid on time?

Set out clear payment terms

The terms you agree with your customers are the starting point for healthy payment times. These payment terms set out when you expect to be paid and form a legally binding agreement with the customer.

You may expect immediate payment on receipt of the invoice. Or you might set out a specific number of days that the customer has to pay the invoice (generally 30, 60, 90 or 120 days, depending on your industry). This is sometimes called 'trade credit' and allows your customers to pay for goods and services at a later, pre-agreed

HELP! I'VE STARTED A BUSINESS

date – helping them spread the cost.

Your payment terms should also include details of any late payment penalties. If the customer doesn't meet your agreed payment times, most businesses will add a 1% to 1.5% monthly late payment fee to the outstanding bill. This acts as a great incentive for the customer to pay the bill, before the penalty fees start mounting up.

Invoice customers as soon as you can

In a business-to-consumer (B2C) environment, your customers will generally pay for their goods and services immediately. But when you're working in the business-to-business (B2B) world, you'll need to send your customer an invoice, asking for the money to be paid.

A customer can't settle their bill until you send them an invoice, so it's vital to send out the invoice as quickly as possible. This minimises the gap between DOING the work and being PAID for the work. In some industries, the project will be broken down into multiple invoices, paid across a period of time. This makes it easier for the customer to pay, and means you (as the supplier) don't have to complete the project before receiving the money you're owed.

Ideally, you want your invoices to go out as early as possible. This allows your payment terms to kick in and makes it easier to predict when cash will be coming into the business.

Be organised about your payment admin

Getting paid is a process – and the more organised you make the process, the quicker the payment will be received. When you send out the invoice, make sure you send it to all the relevant people in the payment chain. This will usually be:

- **Your main contact at the client** – the person in the company who you generally deal with

- **The person who will approve the bill** – the person who will review and green-light the payment

- **The finance team** – the person (or people) who will action the payment and send you the funds.

It's also a good idea to quote any relevant purchase order (PO) numbers that the customer has raised, and to give a very clear description of the work done, or the goods purchased.

Embrace the available payment technology

Invoices used to be hard-copy printed bills, but in the digital age the vast majority of companies will send out e-invoices. Electronic invoices are easy to raise (usually from your accounting software or project management app) and can be emailed out instantly. Doing everything in the digital realm also makes it easier to keep records and keep track of payments.

Many e-invoice systems will also let you add a variety of different payment options for the customer. You could just include your bank details and wait for the customer to make a direct payment to your account. But you can also include payment buttons in the e-invoice that give customers the option to pay via digital payment gateways, like PayPal or GoCardless etc.

Offering more ways to pay makes the whole process more convenient for your customers – and will generally result in faster payment times as a result.

◆◆◆

CHAPTER 16. GETTING IN CONTROL OF YOUR SPENDING

Keeping your business in a positive cashflow position is vital. But you can only do this if your cash inflows (sales revenues and other income) outweigh your cash outflows (overheads, supplier costs and other liabilities like tax costs or loan repayments).

One way to re-balance the cashflow scales is to get in better control of your spending. This process of 'spend management' is all about reviewing your expenses, negotiating better deals with suppliers and getting a razor-sharp focus on reducing your cash outflows.

Review your current suppliers

Once you have a reliable supply chain set up, it's very easy to fall back on using the same suppliers time and time again. But the reality is that there's real value in reviewing the suppliers you're using, so you don't miss out on any better deals.

Prices will go up and down in the marketplace and new suppliers will appear in the market. So, it's worth regularly checking for alternative providers that can offer cheaper rates, better value prices or longer payment terms etc.

Negotiate better prices with your trusted suppliers

You may be happy with the supplier relationships you have, but still want to cut down on your spending. In this scenario, it's well worth negotiating. Very few suppliers will want to lose a valued customer, especially if you're a long-term client who's bringing in reliable revenues. If the relationship is strong enough, they'll be open to negotiating a deal that works for both of you.

See if you can push the prices down, or get discounts for buying in bulk etc. And, if possible, see if you can get them to agree to a trade credit agreement, where you can pay for the goods and services over a longer period of time, to boost your cashflow.

Rein in your expenses

It may sound obvious, but one of the easiest ways to cut your overall expenditure is to be a bit more frugal with your overall spending. Don't overspend on stock, raw materials or services. Just buy what you need to stay operational, and keep a close eye on when new orders will be needed, rather than overspending and using up your available cash.

Where day-to-day spending has got out of hand, you can make a big difference to your expenditure by making small changes to your outgoings. If you sift through your spending with a fine-tooth comb, you'll soon find costs and expenses that can be cut back or stopped entirely. Other cash-saving options could include putting a limit on staff expense cards or canceling unnecessary software and magazine subscriptions etc.

Use a purchase order number system

A purchase order number system makes it easier to keep track of your spending. In essence, any purchase made by the business needs a purchase order (PO) number assigned to it, prior to a member of staff buying anything. This allows you to allocate a budget and track the spending against this particular purchase or project.

Having a PO number also makes it easier to track incoming invoices. Suppliers quote the PO number on their invoice, so you can match the bill to the allocated job and budget.

Use tech to get in control of the numbers

In an ideal world, you want as much oversight over your spending as possible. And with today's cloud accounting software, expenses apps and inventory tools, it's easier than ever to manage your expenses and stay in control of the main numbers.

You can use an expense management system, like Pleo, Soldo or Weel to get better oversight of spending and put yourself back in the expenses driving seat.

◆◆◆

CHAPTER 17.
IMPROVING YOUR
CREDIT SCORE

Your company's credit score is important. To be able to borrow from lenders, or negotiate trade credit with your suppliers, your business needs to prove that it's a low-risk business to lend to.

The major credit agencies will give your business a score, based on its creditworthiness. This score takes into account things like your credit history, your debt profile and the industry you work in. The risk-rating you're given can have a significant impact on your ability to borrow money, so it's sensible to review your credit score and take action to improve it.

But what can you do to bump up that credit score?

Check your SIC code

Your Standard Industry Classification (SIC) code tells the relevant regulatory bodies what industry or sector you trade in. Certain sectors are higher risk than others, so if your SIC code is incorrect, you could be inadvertently bringing down your credit score.

Check the SIC code you're registered with and make sure it properly reflects the sector you work in. It's better to be as specific as possible. By narrowing down your industry classification, you give the credit agencies more information about your business and your risk level.

Improve your payment performance

Paying your creditors on time, and in full, creates a good payment history. The credit agencies will look at how long it takes you to pay your suppliers and main providers. If you're consistently late in paying, that sets a bad precedent and will bump up your risk in the agencies' eyes.

Run a tight accounts payable function and make sure you pay all bills on (or before) the invoice due date. Pay on time, keep your creditors happy and you'll build up a payment history that sets you out as creditworthy.

Don't apply for multiple credit facilities

When cash is in short supply, the temptation is to borrow as much money as you can. But if you apply to multiple lenders for credit facilities, this is bad news for your credit score.

Credit agencies won't look favourably on your need to borrow from multiple sources. In a best-case scenario, it shows that you don't currently have enough liquid cash in the business. In a worst-case scenario, it demonstrates that you're badly organised, poor with managing cashflow and have rising debt in the business.

Consolidate your debt needs into one finance facility, where possible, and deal with one lender. And try to keep your borrowing to a sensible and manageable level.

File the right accounts

In some circumstances, it's possible to file abbreviated accounts. This meets the compliance requirement, but doesn't give the agencies enough detail on your current financial position. And with little to no information to work with, your perceived risk level is likely to increase.

Make sure you're filing full accounts that give the agencies a complete overview of your finances. And ensure you file these accounts on time, so you don't incur any late penalties and give an impression of sloppy financial management.

Avoid any red flags against the company or your directors

Credit agencies are looking for evidence that you're creditworthy, low risk and that your people are 'fit and proper'. Any history of insolvency will act as a red flag and will have a negative impact on the company's credit rating.

If you or your fellow directors have had any previous insolvencies, or have court judgments against you, this will affect your credit score. You can't change the past, but you can make sure you build up a good credit profile and reputation to counteract any of these red flags.

For example:

- Pay on time, every time
- Manage your cash well
- Don't build up unsustainable debt in the business

Meeting these simple goals will have a positive impact on your credit score – and that's good news for the financial future of your business and your growth plans.

◆◆◆

CHAPTER 18. USING FORECASTING TO HELP YOUR DECISION-MAKING

Producing regular management information is one way to help improve your business decision-making. But looking at historical numbers can only tell you so much.

In business, you want to know what the future holds. And to make truly informed decisions about your future strategy, it's important to use forecasting tools to project your data forwards in time. By running projections, based on these historical numbers, and producing detailed forecasts, you can get the best possible view of the road ahead – that's invaluable.

Run regular cashflow forecasts

Positive cashflow is vital to the short, medium and long-term success of your business. Without cash, you simply can't operate the business. Running regular cashflow forecasts helps you overcome this challenge. With detailed projections of your future cashflow, you can spot the cash gaps that lie further down the road, and take action to fill these cashflow holes.

Income can often be unpredictable, especially in challenging economic times. If customers fail to pay an invoice, or suppliers increase their prices, this can all start to eat into your available cash. Using forecasting, you can extrapolate your numbers forward to see which weeks, months or quarters are looking financially tight. With enough prior warning, there's plenty of time to look for short-term funding facilities, or to get proactive with reducing your spending.

Run sales and revenue forecasts

Keeping the business profitable is one of the key foundations of making a success of your enterprise. You want your sales to be stable and your revenues predictable if you're going to generate enough capital to fund your growth plans. And you need to know how those revenues will pan out over the course of the coming financial period.

Revenue forecasts work much like a cashflow forecast. Instead of looking at your future cash position, a revenue forecast gives a projection of your sales and how much revenue is likely to be brought into the business in future weeks and months. With better revenue information, you'll be more on top of your profit targets. You can manage your working capital in a more practical way. And you can improve your ability to invest in new projects, additional staff or funding of the long-term expansion of your business.

Run different scenario plans

What's going to happen to your business in the future? None of us have a crystal ball to predict this future path exactly. But by looking at different possible scenarios, you can run projections to see what the potential outcomes and impacts may be.

These 'What-if scenarios' can be exceptionally useful tools

when thinking about big business decisions. What if there's an economic recession? What if our sales increased by 25%? What if we raised our prices by 10% next quarter? What if we lost a quarter of our customers? By plugging the relevant data into your forecasting engine, you can run these scenarios and see how each option pans out. That's massively useful when the worst (or the best) does happen.

Update your strategy, based on your forecasts

By making the most of your forecasting tools, you give your board, your finance team and your advisers the most insightful data and projections to work from.

A good business plan is designed to flex and evolve to meet the needs of the changing market – and the changing needs of your own business strategy. By making use of your cashflow forecasts, revenue projections and what-if scenario planning, you give yourself the insights needed to update your strategy and your business plan. You can make solid, well-informed decisions and keep yourself one step ahead of your competitors. In the dog-eat-dog world of business, that's a competitive edge that can make a huge difference.

Getting up to speed with the latest forecasting software tools and apps gives you an edge, giving you access to well-executed forecasting and longer-term projections.

◆◆◆

CHAPTER 19. FINDING THE BEST ROUTES TO FINANCE

Every business needs finance to get the initial enterprise off the ground. You may well have borrowed money to fund the initial stages of the business, taking out loans to purchase equipment, lease premises or take on staff.

But when was the last time you reviewed the arrangements or looked at the options for accessing other routes to funding? Are your finance facilities still offering the best interest rates and repayment terms, or are there better deals out there?

Other finance options may be available to help you fund your continuing growth, so taking a look at the current finance market is well worth thinking about.

Refinance your existing loans

It's possible that you already have business loans in place – debts that you'll be repaying over the course of the loan period. Sourcing that initial capital is such an important part of the startup process, and a vital stepping stone in getting your business idea operational. But when was the last time you reviewed these finance arrangements? Could you, in fact, be getting a better deal?

The finance market is always evolving. New challengers will enter the market, new specialist finance products will be introduced and interest rates and repayment schedules will fluctuate and change. You may well have got a great deal on the business loans you took out five years ago – but refinancing these existing loans is likely to have multiple benefits.

You could:

- Consolidate your existing loans into one finance facility

- Lower the interest rate you're currently paying on the loan

- Pay off your loan more quickly, to reduce the underlying debt in the business

- Improve your cashflow position by cutting your repayment expenses

The key point here is that your business finance shouldn't sit still. A loan is not a static debt. You can revisit and refinance your debt, so it works in the best interest of the business.

Look for alternative routes to finance

Traditionally, businesses went to their bank manager when additional funds were needed. But the dynamic in the funding market has changed dramatically in recent years. Due to economic pressures, and the impact of the pandemic, the big banks have scaled back their lending to small businesses. Your high street bank is no longer the first port of call when finance is needed.

On the flipside of this, there are a growing number of alternative lenders, smaller challenger banks and specialist finance providers to choose from. And this has created a wide choice of different finance products to fit the needs of your growth plan.

- If you need new equipment, asset finance is available.

- When you have a short-term cashflow crisis, invoice finance is a good option.

- If larger premises are needed, there are commercial mortgages to consider or bridging loans to make the initial purchase while you source the full capital that's needed.

Check out the available government funding and grant

During the pandemic, many businesses made use of the emergency funding that governments made available. But don't forget that government funding isn't just something that's available during an emergency.

The state will generally offer all kinds of different enterprise schemes to encourage investment in new and growing companies. This could mean having access to funding schemes, government-secured loans or even government grants. Unlike a loan, grants generally don't need to be repaid, so making use of local government grants is a great way to boost your capital without having a negative impact on the company's debt position.

Explore the tax reliefs that are open to your business

Another element of government-back financial support is the use of tax reliefs. One of your major expenses as a business will be paying your corporation tax (CT) bill. But there are usually various tax reliefs available to help you reduce your CT bill and reinvest that saved money back into the business. Careful use of these reliefs can make a big difference to your finances.

For example, many countries offer some form of research and

development (R&D) tax relief scheme. To encourage businesses to innovate and invest in R&D, the government will offer a relief against the company's expenditure on operational R&D costs. This will usually mean either reducing your CT liability, or giving you a cash payment against your R&D expenses.

Choosing the right routes to funding and finance will be vital to your long-term success as a business – so work closely with your advisers and think carefully about your choices.

◆◆◆

CHAPTER 20.
NURTURING
YOUR CUSTOMER
RELATIONSHIPS

The stability of your business isn't just based on sound finances. Forming rock-solid foundations comes from having a solid customer base and building long-lasting relationships with your end users. To achieve this, you need to work hard on nurturing these relationships.

But how do you keep your customers happy and satisfied? And what are the best ways to build and maintain a trusted and beneficial relationship with everyone in your sales book?

Here are a few fundamentals for keeping those relationships sweet…

Great communication with your customers

Any good relationship is based on honest and open communication. So, it's important to have the best possible channels for two-way communication, feedback and promotion. Talking directly to customers, and allowing them to communicate with you, opens up a dialogue and gets a conversation started. And when customers are willing to have that conversation, you can be confident that they'll be open to your marketing, emails and other points of contact.

Key ways to achieve this could include:

● **Make use of the full range of digital channels** – some customers will check out your website before making a purchase. Others will follow your updates on social media. Some will prefer email newsletters and updates. Find out what they prefer and use the channels that have the best feedback, engagement and conversation rates.

● **Put some effort into your social media channels** – social media platforms are a great way to communicate directly with your customer base. But you need to make the time to post regularly, reply to queries and respond to praise (and criticism too).

● **Know your customers inside out** – where possible, getting to know your customers face-to-face is invaluable. Digital channels are incredibly useful, but they can't replace chatting with your customers in person. Hold customer events, go to trade conferences and ask your team to represent your brand in a friendly and engaging way.

Ask for feedback and comments

For your products and/or services to improve, you need honest feedback from your customers. Ask for feedback on your delivery, your customer service, waiting times and prices etc. And, crucially, find out how you can do better. The root of any product development lies in knowing what your customers want, and how their needs are evolving. If you can gather those opinions and information from your end users, that's invaluable data on which to base your decisions.

If you're selling a physical product, ask the customer to answer a few quick questions when completing their warranty details online. If you're selling a service, then follow up any project with a 'How did we do?' survey that asks for high-level feedback on their experience. The more you ask, the more you will know – and that knowledge really is power in the business world.

Keep customers in the loop
with new developments

When you're starting your next round of product development, stop for a moment and think about who this product is for. Ultimately, you're designing and evolving something to meet the specific needs of a certain customer demographic. So, who better to ask about the direction of your updated product or service? Talk to the end user and ask them what they want.

As a business, it's very easy to get lost in the internal, in-house viewpoint of your development. A new idea could result in what's seen as an excellent new product feature – but have you asked the end user if they want this feature? Aiming for a positive customer experience (CX) and meeting your customers' needs should ALWAYS be your core aim. So, get your end users involved in the development process and your beta testing of products.

Reward your best customers
with perks and benefits

We all like to know that our custom is valued. When you form an attachment to a brand, and give the company your hard-earned cash, you want to know that this is appreciated. One way to make your customers feel valued in this way is to offer them perks and benefits – something that only your long-term customers will have access to.

This could mean:

- Giving valued customers early access to new products or services

- Offering customers a healthy discount on purchases, or giving away freebies

- Starting an 'Introduce a friend' scheme, where the introducing customer gets a gift

- Running events for existing customers to build on their feelings of community

The more you can do to make each and every customer feel special, the more chance you have of building a great relationship – and turning these people into advocates for your brand.

◆◆◆

CHAPTER 21. BOOSTING YOUR SALES, MARKETING AND ONLINE PRESENCE

Getting a startup off the ground takes a big focus on sales and marketing. But has your marketing activity grown to meet the challenges of being a larger and more stable company?

When you scale up your business and operations, your sales and marketing must scale at the same rate. To reach a greater number of customers and achieve higher sales, it's necessary to raise awareness of the brand – and that means upping your sales and marketing activity.

Expand your sales and marketing activity

Scaling up is all about 'hypergrowth' – rapid annual growth of the business that exceeds 40%. When you move beyond organic growth to hypergrowth, your sales and marketing activity has to take a similar leap in productivity. And with digital now such a vital channel, your online activity will also need a boost, so you can make the most of online sales and e-commerce etc.

Hitting your growth and sales targets means running more campaigns. Targeting a wider audience. And aiming to convert customers at a faster rate. To do this, you don't just need a new strategy for the business. You also need more people, bigger sales and marketing teams and systems that can grow and scale as the business expands.

Update your sales and marketing systems

If you don't already have one, look at a system that connects your customer relationship management (CRM) database with a modern sales and marketing system. By getting organised, you make it easier to manage your supercharged levels of activity. And you also have more oversight of your sales enquiries, marketing campaigns and customer information.

Cloud-based software platforms like Hubspot or ActiveCampaign give you the tools, resources and customer data you need to take your campaigns to the next level. Keep detailed information about customers and targets. Run large-scale campaigns, both online and offline. And run reports and analytics to see where you're hitting your targets and where more work is needed.

Branch out into new channels

Once you've secured funding for your scale-up strategy, your overall sales and marketing budget should get a boost. Where cash restraints have potentially held you back in the past, now you've got the financial resources to try new things and spread your promotional wings.

Growing your audience is key, so think about how you can achieve this.

Why not try:

- **TV and radio advertising** – mass media advertising is a BIG step, with even bigger costs. But getting your brand on TV or radio takes you into the next level when it comes to brand awareness and overall understanding of your products and services.

- **A wider focus on social media** – you're probably already posting on the standard social channels, like Facebook and Twitter. But extending out into platforms like TikTok and YouTube can bag you a whole new audience. Having a community manager and social team will greatly extend your ability to build a solid following on social media.

- **Attending more industry events** – get your sales team out in the field so they can meet more people in your sector. Going to big conferences, seminars and events expands your network of targets and gets the brand name known within the right inner circles. Online interaction is great, but nothing replaces talking face-to-face.

- **Sponsoring events or teams** – many large industry conferences will be looking for sponsorship partners. It's a large expense, but it does guarantee you certain privileges and access to attendees. Sponsoring sports or leisure events is another option, as is sponsoring an athlete or sports team and getting your logo on their kit.

- **Partnering with other organisations** – Coming together with a business or organisation that compliments your own offering can expand your reach and cut down on some of the costs. If you're a sports-shoe manufacturer, partnering with a gym makes sense. If you're a book publisher, working with a literacy social enterprise is a good idea.

The key here is to step outside of your comfort zone and reach a bigger (or newer) audience. So think outside the box and use your new resources wisely.

Create new brand messaging

When you first started out, your 'We've got an awesome new widget!' messaging got you off the ground with new customers and targets. But as the product has evolved and your brand has expanded, that initial tagline and messaging probably no longer fit the bill.

Work with external creative agencies to come up with new brand stories, new messaging and a clearer brand identity for what is now a much larger business. Yes, this will cost you plenty in agency fees, but it's an investment that helps you refine and turbo-charge your external brand.

Be smart with your sales and marketing activity

Focusing on your return on investment (ROI) is critical. No-one wants to see expensive above-the-line campaigns bombing and wasting huge amounts of cash. Do your customer research, run analytics and use the invaluable customer data you've accrued to create the best possible impact from your sales and marketing.

Look back at your engagement figures, conversion rates and sales numbers, and see where you're hitting the nail on the head (and where you're just bashing your thumb with a hammer).

If you're starting your scale-up journey and want to supercharge your sales and marketing, there's real value in working with experts in the field. Connect you with agencies, consultants and campaign experts, so you're ready to start the next chapter in your brand's evolution.

◆◆◆

CHAPTER 22. MAKING THE MOST OF DIGITAL AND CLOUD

Transforming into a digital business sets the best possible infrastructure for your future growth. And, as your business scales, the benefits of going digital will start to become obvious.

Running your key business processes in the cloud and using the latest digital software and apps adds to both your efficiency and your productivity. And, most importantly, digital systems are designed to scale with you as your enterprise grows and the need for resources increases.

Here are some of the big reasons for taking the plunge and diving into digital.

Automate your manual processes to increase efficiency

A scalable business has to systemise its processes and procedures. If your business model is still tied to manual processes and a system that only exists in the owner's head, you'll eventually come up against a capacity brick wall. Systemising and automating your processes is a fundamental step when you make the jump to digital.

Look at every internal and external step in your operations and write down how these systems work. Note down each task, who actions what and how the whole system links in with the next step in your operational chain. If there are opportunities to automate a step, automate it. Many business apps now include artificial intelligence (AI) features that can chase up unpaid invoices, send automated replies to customers in live chats, or take automatic payments etc.

Work in the cloud to stay more connected

Since the start of the 2020 pandemic, the world has seen a quantum shift to remote working – and that's only been possible because of cloud technology. Instead of working from local applications on our laptops or office-based servers, most tech-savvy businesses now use cloud-based apps that are accessible anywhere you have an internet connection.

Switching to cloud-based systems is a game-changer. You and your team are no longer tied to a physical office and can be productive from any WiFi-enabled location. That could be your home, your customer's warehouse, your regional office or your local coffee shop. And the benefits aren't just limited to remote working. With your applications and databases in the cloud, you can access customer information, sales data or financial numbers wherever you happen to be. Everything is securely backed up and available at the press of a button – that's an invaluable benefit if you want to be flexible, connected and scalable as a business.

Create your own custom app stack

Your business systems and software no longer have to remain static and based on the office server. By combining a business and accounting platform like Xero, MYOB, QuickBooks or Sage with your own choice of business apps, you can create a truly tailored 'app stack'.

Apps use an API (application programming interface) to connect with each other, share data and form a larger business system. This can include apps to:

- Manage and automate your bookkeeping and accounting tasks

- Send out e-invoices to your customers to speed up payments

- Take automated payments and reconcile your transactions

- Automatically chase late-paying customers and carry out credit control duties

- Project-manage your operations and provide detailed reporting

- Manage your job utilisation and time spent on each project

- Keep a detailed real-time inventory of your products

- Send out marketing campaigns and social media posts to your audience

- Interact more closely with your end customers and learn their habits

Record and track your business data

App integrations and a customer app stack don't just improve your productivity. Because your apps are connected via APIs and are sharing your business data, you also have access to a wealth of data, information and reporting features.

Look in detail at your cashflow, expenses and spending to improve your cash position. Take a deep dive into your sales and marketing information to find out who your best (and most profitable) customers are. Run projections and 'What if…' scenarios, based on your historical data to forecast the future path of the business. There are plenty of ways to make use of this bountiful data to help you review, understand and improve your performance as a company.

A business in the pre-computer age would have had very little information on which to base its decision-making. Annual accounts, cashflow statements and some basic management information would have been available, but there was very little real-time data to refer to.

In the digital age, you can literally see every aspect of your company's performance in real-time – and, in some cases, in the future as well. That's a game-changer in so many ways, and something every business owner should be using to improve strategy, financial management, customer experience and business decision-making.

To summarise, a digital business:

1. Creates systems that are integrated and connected
2. Shares and records all your business data
3. Reviews, analyses and finds insights in your business information
4. Connects with your customers in more meaningful ways
5. Makes better-informed business decisions, as a result

If you're serious about scaling up, it's a no-brainer to go digital. Switching to cloud-based app stack gives you everything you need to become a modern, digital business.

◆◆◆

CHAPTER 23. THE IMPORTANCE OF BUSINESS DEVELOPMENT

Business development is one of the most important areas of focus for any ambitious business.

If you want your business to grow, that's going to mean having a razor-sharp focus on new opportunities and strategies. That could mean exploring new markets, or nurturing new partnerships. It might mean diversifying to create new revenue streams, or coming up with new ideas to boost your profitability. But, ultimately, good business development comes down to having good ideas – ideas that broaden your reach, sales, revenues and external relationships.

As the founder or CEO, it's important to put business development at the top of your to-do list.

Put time aside for business development

Business opportunities don't just appear out of thin air (sadly). To come up with an opportunity for a business partnership, or to bring in a big new client, you're going to have to do some serious work. So, it's a good idea to put business development (BD) time aside in your diary.

By blocking out time to devote to BD, you can step away from the everyday operational tasks and get into a more creative and objective mindset. Where do you want the business to be in six months? What do you need to do to achieve this goal? Are there relationships you could build to bring this plan to life? Asking these questions and getting a more concrete idea of the answers will form the basis for your BD plan – and that's the route map you can then follow.

Work on your BD plan and strategy

Once you have some positive BD ideas to work with, it's important to get your goals and your strategy down into some form of plan. As with any kind of growth initiative, your BD activity needs to be well planned, so you have a clear idea of what you want to achieve.

Give each new strategic idea a clear timeline and assign jobs, activities and roles to the relevant people in the team. Cost out each project and assign a budget. That way you can be sure that you're getting the best return on your investment (both financially and from a time perspective).

Most importantly, track your progress against your BD goals. Agree on a target, set a date and measure your progress and performance against that timeline.

Build relationships with potential partners and customers

Relationships lie at the heart of your BD activity. You might be getting to know the executive team at a possible new partner's company. Or you may be reaching out to a new customer audience with a brand-new product. Getting to understand what makes these people tick is so important to warming them up as a potential partner, customer or supplier.

Trust is the real key here. People are more likely to engage with your business when they trust you as people and as a brand. So, spending time nurturing relationships and networking with other businesspeople and targets is time well spent.

Record, track and analyse your BD performance

With your goals, targets and timelines locked in, you're ready to start putting this BD plan into action. But to know if you're making headway, it's a good idea to track your performance.

If you're using project management software or a client relationship management (CRM) app, it's easy to add notes, record your progress and tick off the key actions in the project. You can put the financial reporting tools in your accounting software to good use. Track cashflow for the project, look for increases in revenue and monitor your sales and marketing expenses etc.

Get ambitious with your BD ideas

No business stands still. Your aims and goals as the owner will change. Your market will evolve and new competitors will appear. Economic conditions and business opportunities will change. To keep your business at the cutting edge, it's vital to keep your BD focus alive and well.

Remember to:

- Define your goals and make it clear what you want the business to achieve

- Align your BD activity with the company's main growth plan

- Log your ideas and potential opportunities and add them to your BD plan

- Warm up your targets and potential partners and keep notes on your progress

- Track your BD performance against your targets, budgets, revenues and timelines

- Keep revisiting your plan and flexing your BD activity to the current market.

Expanding your business development activity starts by setting some achievable targets and having a solid plan to work from. From there, the sky's the limit.

◆◆◆

CHAPTER 24. HOW AN ACCOUNTANT SUPPORTS YOUR BUSINESS DEVELOPMENT

You're used to an accountant looking after the financial side of your business. But a good accountant can be equally at home advising you on the strategic side of your company, including the importance of business development as a vital part of your growth plan.

Business development (BD) is what helps your company move from slow, organic growth to fast-paced, hypergrowth. And it's only by putting the right drive and expertise behind your BD that you can turn your strategic ideas into real success stories.

So, what can your accountant do to help you achieve this?

Talk to you about your strategic goals

The starting point for any kind of BD activity is to pin down your goals and aims as a business. When you know what you want to achieve over the coming months, it's far easier to define a strategy for success. And that's easier to do when you talk to an objective adviser.

An adviser can sit in on your board meetings, talk to your executive team and get a real handle on what makes the business tick. And, armed with this knowledge, they can work with you to drive the direction of your BD and find the best opportunities for you to focus on.

Help you create a clear BD strategy and plan

Having a defined set of BD goals is a good starting point. But to put this all into action in a productive way, you're going to need a comprehensive plan for your BD projects.

An experienced accountant knows the best routes to take, the budgets that will be needed and the right tactics for bringing in more contracts, sales and partnerships. By working closely with your adviser, you can put these strategies into a clear plan, and link each item to agreed timescales. This gives you a BD route map to follow and action.

Introduce you to a broader network of business partners

Accountants work with a wide range of businesses across many different sectors, industries and niches. If you can get an introduction to their client network, you'll find yourself becoming part of a supportive community of like-minded business owners – and that's excellent news when looking for advice, support and new partnerships.

Whether it's attending a local conference, an online webinar or an in-house client event, you're going to meet new people, share new ideas and make the right connections. This is a great way to build alliances and work together with other local businesses. And when you're well-connected, you set the very best foundations for your future BD activity.

Provide better routes to funding and investment

Whatever goals you've set for your BD projects, it's likely that you'll need additional funding to fund this activity. Investing in your expansion, or new partnerships, is vital to getting a good return on your BD, so great access to finance is a definite bonus.

A well-connected accountant will be able to advise you on the most appropriate funding channels and how you can use these facilities to finance your BD plans. They'll also be able to link you up with banks, lenders and business finance specialists – so you get the advice and finance you need to bring your BD to life.

Help you track and measure your BD performance

Meeting your BD targets takes time – and a whole lot of dedication. Measuring your BD performance over time helps you stay on track and gives you a good indication of how well you're tracking against your planned progress.

As a finance professional, your accountant will be able to create the reporting and metrics you need, so you have clear data to track your progress over time. You can log your activity in your project management system, or your client relationship management (CRM) software, and keep clear notes on contacts made, relationships built and targets converted etc.

If you want to get more from your BD, partnering with an experienced adviser will set you on the right path – so you have real drive, experience and impetus behind your BD strategies.

◆◆◆

CHAPTER 25. KNOWING WHAT YOUR CUSTOMER ACTUALLY WANTS

The increase in digital business systems has opened up forensic ways of understanding your customer base. That's a huge bonus when you're aiming to build better connections, relationships and experiences with your audience.

Knowing what your customer wants is a fundamental piece of knowledge for any successful business to get to grips with. And when you're running a modern, digital business there's an overwhelming wealth of customer and sales data and analytics at your disposal – making it easier than ever to dig down into the needs and habits of your end user.

Detailed CRM records and customer notes

If you're not using a customer relationship management (CRM) platform to manage your customer information, the question has to be 'Why not?'. A CRM system becomes the heart of your customer management, business development and marketing activity, allowing you to log activity, keep notes and record progress throughout the sales pipeline.

The more information you have about your valued customers, the more you can do to meet their needs and deliver the perfect customer experience. And by maximising your use of this customer data, you can tightly focus your marketing campaigns and do more to make every customer feel understood, valued and (most importantly) satisfied.

Drilled-down sales records

Keeping tabs on your sales activity is central to any business model. In an ideal world, you want regular, repeatable sales from a loyal customer base. But sales activity can be hard to predict, especially when you're setting ambitious sales targets for your team to hit.

Having sales records and data at your fingertips has two key benefits:

1. You know how sales have fared in the past
2. You know how sales may pan out in the future

Being able to run forecasts, based on your historic sales data gives you a stable foundation on which to build your future sales targets. It's a solid projection, based on real business data. But this data also gives you an encyclopaedic overview of what your customers have been buying.

This sales data helps you understand:

- Which products/services your customers want to spend their money on

- Which specific products/services are failing to convert

- Which points in the year will have peaks and troughs in sales

- When it's the right time to invest in more sales and marketing activity

This is all gold dust when it comes to planning out your strategy, assigning your sales and marketing resources and building engagement with your core audiences.

Marketing analytics and customer touch points

Marketing is a vital part of getting your brand message out into the world. Today's digital marketing and email platforms make it easier than ever to see the results and analytics from your marketing campaign and to answer meaningful questions about the outcomes:

- How many customers clicked through from your call-to-action?

- How many click-throughs were converted into sales?

- How many views did your latest blog post get?

- Who opened your latest email campaign?

- Which one of your customer segments is most engaged?

With the marketing analytics that digital systems can provide, you know the answers to all these questions. That's incredibly helpful when working out which campaigns delivered a good return-on-investment (ROI), which customer groups are most engaged and where your marketing is hitting the mark (or not, as the case may be).

Social media interactions and feedback

Social media platforms, like Twitter, Facebook, LinkedIn and

TikTok, give your business a cheap and effective way of getting your brand messages out to a wider audience. But unlike above-the-line advertising and mass marketing, social media is a two-way communication channel. It's a conduit for your customers and followers to message you, ask questions and give you feedback – and in that sense, it's a vital way of understanding your customers' needs.

As you scale and grow, an increased focus on social media will be vital. Hiring a social media manager, or working with a social media agency, helps you broaden out your social activity and really engage with your followers. Reply to queries, placate frustrated customers and share your latest news and updates. If you can be present and engaging in the social space, that's going to help you cement your bond with these valued customers.

Online customer feedback and star ratings

The acid test of your customer experience is simple: are your customers happy? Satisfied and happy customers become amazing advocates for your brand. But disgruntled and unhappy customers can quickly undo the good work you've done in building up your brand.

In the online age, bad news spreads incredibly quickly, and customer feedback, reviews and trust scores are a vital part of your brand's equity. A series of terrible reviews for your cafe on a platform like TripAdviser can cause serious damage. So, it's important that you engage with these reviews, run customer surveys and listen carefully to any customer feedback.

Ultimately, delighting your customer is your key aim as a business owner. Using your ears and listening to the feedback you get is integral to understanding what your customers want.

If you want to hit your growth targets, that's far easier to achieve when you know the needs of your customers and can accurately target your sales, marketing and social activity.

◆◆◆

CHAPTER 26.
BUILDING YOUR
BRAND TO CREATE
A COMPETITIVE
ADVANTAGE

If your company can be bigger, better and more dominant in your sector, that's good news for your hypergrowth target. But in a crowded marketplace, it can be difficult to make your products and services stand out clearly from the competition.

A key way to do this is to focus on building brand awareness and turning your existing customers and targets into advocates for your brand.

Sounds simple, doesn't it? Creating that competitive advantage won't always be easy, but it is key to carving out a niche and scaling up to meet your customers' needs.

Clearly define your brand values

As a big player in your sector, it's important to communicate what your brand stands for. This means being transparent about your company vision and the core values you will operate by. Once your brand values have been established, use them to guide every business decision, from marketing to operations; e.g. if sustainability is a core value, this must be reflected in the choices you make on suppliers, packaging, distribution and the causes you associate with.

When your company values jump out from your marketing and customer interactions, it makes it easier to resonate with the right customers – and that's a key part of building good relationships

Create a memorable personality for your brand

Think about the personality you associate with your favourite brands. Apple is cutting edge, aspirational and techy, while Ben & Jerry's ice cream is kooky, laid-back and reflects the hippy roots of its founders. How do you want your customers to feel about *your* brand?

Should the personality of your brand sound professional, expert and high class? Or would your audience engage better with a personality that's warm, approachable and more friendly? Whatever you decide, your tone of voice and the personality of your brand has to be consistent across all channels. Make sure your website, marketing collateral and social media posts all have a uniform feel and represent the brand in a way which can be quickly identified.

Have a recognisable brand identity

Part of creating brand recognition is having a clear visual appearance for the brand. The logo you use, the style of your web content and the way your packaging is designed all help to make your brand more recognisable to a broader audience.

Be creative with your design and decide on a 'visual identity' with colours, fonts and imagery that reflect your chosen personality as a brand. The human brain processes images much faster than text, and that's why good imagery and design is so important. If you can commission the images (design or photography) yourself, the result will feel more authentic, but stock image libraries offer lots of choice too. Avoid cliched images that don't reflect your brand and, wherever possible, aim to create a unique identity that stands out in your marketplace.

Differentiate your brand from the competition

Does your product stand out from other similar products offered by your competitors? The more unique you can make your offering, the more likely it is that your brand will be the one that people turn to. You can differentiate by features, price, customer service etc. to make sure you're the stand-out option for customers in this market.

There's also the option of creating your own niche, where competitors are few and far between. To protect this dominance, it's important to maintain your high-quality service, to work closely with your customers and to remain at the cutting edge of the specialism.

Know your price and how it fits customers' needs

Price can be a real differentiator, so you need to be aware how your prices compare to those of your competitors. Is your product cheaper than others? Or are you pitching your price at the top end of the market? The more competitive your price point is, and the more it's linked to your unique value, the easier it will be to carve out a competitive advantage.

Be clear about whether you're offering a premium, standard or economy product, and how this price point fits with your customers' expectations of the brand. Offering good value for money will be an important draw, so keep an eye on the competitiveness of your prices.

Build a valued community
of brand advocates

Do you have a strong network amongst your customer base, or is a competitor gradually winning market share and undermining your supremacy as the market leader? This needs to be regularly reviewed and assessed.

A focus on customer relationships is vital. Offer discounts and unique offers to your long-standing customers to keep them on side. Ask for comments and feedback, so you know what customers want from the brand. And turn your existing customers into advocates for the brand – so they get out in the real world and refer you to the rest of their network.

◆◆◆

CHAPTER 27: TRADING IN A DIFFERENT COUNTRY

Once you've built a stable customer base in your home country, you may start to think about widening your niche and trading in new countries and territories.

To do this successfully, you'll need to do your research. This means talking to your accountant, advisers and other business owners in your network, so you don't enter the market without enough preparation. With the right planning and organisation, you set the best possible foundations for moving into a brand-new international market.

Create an export plan

When you take the big step of going international, having a plan is going to help immeasurably. Writing an export plan gives you a route map to follow and helps to explain to investors, funding providers and your existing home team WHY you're looking to expand out into a new country.

As a starting point:

- Explain your business reasons for trading in this new territory

- Give a detailed explanation of your supply chain and how it will work

- Outline your strategy for finding customers, making sales and generating revenue

- Summarise the costs of going international and where you hope to find the funding

- Give an overview of the company's current financial health and cashflow position

- Set your initial targets for the first year and your timescales for achieving them.

Check if you need an export licence

It's possible that you'll need an export licence in your home country to trade over country borders. This will depend on what goods you're exporting, whether they are on any controlled lists and whether there's an existing trade agreement with your target county.

Free trade agreements (FTAs) may exist between your home country and your export country, reducing or removing some of the regulatory hurdles required to trade between those two territories. For example, prior to Brexit, the UK had access to all FTAs negotiated by the European Union. Now that the UK has left the EU, these FTAs have been removed – although the UK does now have trading agreements with a few select overseas territories.

Understand your VAT/GST liability

According to the OECD, 170 countries and territories have some form of Value-Added Tax (VAT) or Goods and Services Tax (GST). These consumption taxes are added to non-essential goods and are paid by the consumer as part of the price they pay at the till.

Knowing whether you'll need to charge and pay VAT/GST in your new territory is an important consideration. Countries will charge VAT/GST at different rates, on different goods and services. So, it's important to talk to a specialist who can advise you on how to deal with VAT/GST when trading across borders in your new country.

Move to multi-currency accounting software

If you've only traded in your home nation, your finances will have been managed in a single currency up to this point. Unless you're operating in a trading block with one standard currency (like the EU), the likelihood is that your new export location will use a different currency.

Whether your new location trades in US dollars, euros or Japanese yen, your accounting software needs to be able to deal with transactions in your home currency and your new international currency. Most of the major cloud accounting platforms will offer a multi-currency subscription, giving you the ability to account in multiple currency types.

Find the best way to get paid in a new currency

When you make your first sales in your international territory, you'll also need a way to take payment in this new currency. With cashless card transactions now so common in many parts of the world, this is less of an issue than it used to be. However, you will need a bank account that uses your new currency and some means of converting funds into your home currency.

International bank accounts with foreign exchange (forex) capabilities make this easier. Providers like Wise Business, OFX or Revolut, give you the option to collect payments in one currency and then export it in your home currency. This makes the forex process much simpler and also much more cost-effective, with rates usually far lower than those your high-street bank would charge for forex transactions.

Market your brand to a new audience

A key step will be marketing your brand to consumers in this new country, or finding other businesses to sell to directly. Remember, you're starting from scratch when it comes to brand awareness and advocacy, so it's important to do as much research as possible.

Questions to ask include:

- Is there a need for your goods and services in this new market?

- Who are the current brand leaders and your direct competitors?

- How will you differentiate your goods in a crowded market ?

- Do you have the resources to create marketing content in a second language?

Remember to also check on cultural sensitivities in your new country. Do you understand the cultural, social and religious differences between your home nation and your new territory? Using the wrong words, phrases or colours in your marketing could be disastrous, so learn as much as possible about your new country and get to know the local traditions.

Going international is a significant step for your business. But if you get it right, there's potential for worldwide success and a global reputation for you and your company.

◆◆◆

CHAPTER 28.
BEING A GREEN
AND SUSTAINABLE
BUSINESS

We all know that climate change is a huge problem for the world at large. Helping to lower our carbon footprint and live more sustainable lives is key to lowering carbon emissions and bringing down the rapidly rising average temperatures we're seeing around the world.

But is your business doing everything it can to support a sustainability agenda? And are there simple, straightforward ways to reduce your negative impact on the planet?

The need to tackle global warming

Stopping global warming is probably the biggest challenge currently facing humanity. But are you fully aware of the part your company can play in reducing global warming?

Many business owners realise the importance of being greener and sustainable as an organisation. But the vast majority don't know where to start and still require more guidance around how they can meet their sustainability

Key areas of sustainability to focus on can include:

- **Your use of paper** – are you still printing out agendas, speaker notes and letters on paper? Paper production involves a huge amount of natural resources and has a negative impact on our environment. By moving to paperless business processes, you reduce your impact and make your operations more eco-friendly.

- **Your reliance on plastics** – are you using plastics as part of your production process, or offering single-use plastics as part of your office refreshments? The world makes millions of tonnes of plastics annually across the world, but these plastics last for decades, don't biodegrade and are gradually polluting every area of the planet. Reducing your reliance on plastics and opting for biodegradable alternatives goes a long way to improving your environmental impact as a business.

- **The eco-credentials of your suppliers** – have you reviewed your suppliers' eco-credentials and opted for the most sustainable supplies? If your business is following a green strategy, this can easily be underlined if your suppliers are not managing their carbon emissions. Where possible, choose local suppliers so you can reduce the distance your supplies travel and the carbon footprint they create.

- **The impact of your own operations** – are you analysing the impact of your own manufacturing processes or service provision on the planet? Setting yourself green targets as part of your corporate social responsibility (CSR) strategy will help you to gain better oversight. Choose environmentally friendly materials, manufacturing methods, logistics and packaging. And track and record your progress against these green targets.

- **The impact of commuting** – do you really need your entire workforce to be operating from one central HQ in the city or town centre? The greater the distance that your employees travel, and the more frequently they do this, the higher their individual carbon footprints will be. Supporting a move to hybrid working allows your employees to work from a mix of different locations, limiting the need for a daily commute.

- **Your reliance on long-distance travel** – Are you taking long-haul flights and driving long distances to a client's HQ when a video meeting would do the job? International plane travel has a significant impact on the environment, as does using an internal combustion engine (ICE) car. If you can hold remote meetings with clients, this greatly reduces your personal and corporate impact on global warming.

Reviewing and updating your sustainability strategy

This is not an exhaustive list of ways to tackle sustainability in your business. But it will help to kickstart your thinking. That's vital as we face the ongoing challenge of climate change.

As business owners, we all have a responsibility to play our part in reducing carbon emissions, acting more sustainably and doing our best to be good global citizens.

◆◆◆

CHAPTER 29. HAVE YOU ACHIEVED YOUR GOALS FOR THE BUSINESS?

Founding, managing and growing a business is a BIG commitment. For most business owners, it will take years to build a customer following, turn a profit and create a truly scalable business. It's a journey that can sometimes be pressurised, stressful and risky – and a large number of startups won't make it beyond the first two years, because of this.

But when your plan really does come together, there is the chance of real success, a lasting legacy and a business that delivers on your initial dream.

So, how do you know when you've truly achieved your goals for the business?

Has the business met its growth targets and scaled up as intended?

Hopefully, the business will have grown over the course of the past few years. You'll have seen your business idea grow from being a fledgling startup, to an established business and on to become a scaled-up, ambitious enterprise with a solid customer base.

If you've met these growth targets, then you know you're on solid ground as a business. Your idea clearly has legs and you're delivering a product and/or service that your customers see as valuable – and which they're willing to part with their hard-earned cash to purchase.

Are you running a profitable enterprise that's in good financial shape?

Running a tight financial ship is crucial. 'Cash is King!', as the old adage goes, and you need solid revenues, positive cashflow and good liquidity to keep your business ticking over.

In the early days of being a startup, cash will have been tight. And your own personal income as a founder and director will probably have been scarce too. But as the business has become more established, you should have found that your business revenue became more stable and predictable. Your own personal wealth should also have followed this same reliable pattern.
If the business has a solid balance sheet, great cashflow and meets your intended profit targets, you're onto a good thing – and can be sure that your financial position is in good shape.

Do you have a stable customer base who say good things about you?

Without customers, you don't have a viable business. And finding your first customers was probably a significant turning point in your startup journey. A good customer base brings with it the bonus of new sales, fresh revenues and a business that can actually turn a profit. But having customers isn't just about making money

When customers engage with you and buy your goods and services, that comfirms your original faith in your business idea. You're providing something they value and want to purchase, and you're also building a community of like-minded people who all think your brand is great. That's more than just a sound financial move. It's also part of you achieving your original vision and leaving behind the kind of legacy you intended.

Do you have a team who can operate the business without you?

In the early days, you'll probably have become a jack (or jill) or all trades. You'll have run the sales and marketing campaigns, taken care of all the main operational tasks and dealt with the many invoicing, accounting and bookkeeping tasks. Turn the clock forward, and you probably have a team of people around you to take care of these jobs – but could they function without you?

This is really the acid test of whether you've scaled and succeeded. If the business is still reliant on you, personally, you have a problem. To be a saleable proposition, a business needs to function effectively without the founder. If not, you'll never be in a position to sell up. To make this possible, you need a team of engaged and talented people around you – people who share your vision and talents and who can keep the ship on an even course, even once the original captain has set sail on fresh, new adventures.

Do you feel you've achieved what you wanted to achieve?

In your formative years as a founder, you'll have sat down to draw up a startup plan. In that plan you'll have outlined a clear vision for what this business was going to achieve.

This vision might have been:

- To scale up over five years, sell-up and make a million for you to retire on

- To deliver a new kind of technical widget and make it the global standard

- To help your target audience improve their lives, helped by your product/service

- To provide the income needed for you to live your desired lifestyle

- To plough your profits back into the local community and be a force for good

We all have different goals, and whether they are financial, personal or moral comes down to the individual. The important thing at this point is to assess whether you've actually met the vision that you set out to achieve. If your aim was to sell for a profit and then retire, are you ready to do this? If the goal was to become a household name and move your sector forward, do your customer engagement figures and market share stats reflect this?

Deep down, only you and your fellow founders know whether you've truly met your intended goal. But if the consensus is that you aced it, then it's time to think about the future.

What's the next chapter in your business story?

If you can answer yes to all five of these questions, then congratulations! You've built a successful, stable and profitable business.

But what do you do now? Do you continue to plough this fertile furrow and live off the profits? Do you find a buyer for the existing business and start on your next business idea? Or do you sell up and look at retirement and enjoying the benefits of your money and lifestyle?

The choice is yours, but it's a good idea to talk to your advisers (and other business owners) before you make what is, essentially, a life-changing decision.

◆◆◆

PART 3 – EXITING THE BUSINESS

CHAPTER 30. SETTING YOUR GOALS FOR A BUSINESS EXIT

Every business has a finite lifespan. Some may last for decades, and others only a few years. But as the owner of a business, the life of your business is likely to be strongly aligned with your own life goals and personal plans for the future.

When the time comes to sell up, it's important to know what your goals are for the sale. Are you looking to retire? Or do you have a burning ambition to start a new venture?

Define your exact goals from the sale of the business

At the point of planning an exit, you need to think carefully about WHY you're selling up and WHAT you want to achieve. This is a huge change in your life, your business career and the fortunes of your company and employees. So, any sale needs to be properly thought through.

Ask yourself what your true goals are from this exit:

- Do you want to retire, ease the pressure and enjoy your golden years?

- Has your business journey come to an end and you need a new challenge?

- Do you need to free up your capital to invest in other business or personal projects?

- Is there a worthy successor who's itching to jump into the hot seat?

Whatever the motivation for a business exit may be, be sure to consider your options and decide on some concrete end goals.

Who is going to take over the business?

To be able to sell the business, you obviously need a buyer. Business sales are rarely a simple process and by putting the company on the market you're opening yourself up to a complicated process of negotiation, financial agreements and legal wrangling.

Knowing who will take over the business can be difficult to predict, but you do have several options when it comes to the end outcome.

For example, you could:

- Sell the business outright to a new owner and remove yourself from the company

- Sell the business but remain on as chairperson or a non-executive director (NED)

- Merge the business with a sympathetic competitor to aid their growth

- Agree to a partial or complete acquisition from a competitor or private equity firm

- Pass the business on to the next generation of your family

- Agree to a management buyout from your existing team.

Outline how the sale proceeds will be used

Once any sale, merger or acquisition is complete, you'll be on the receiving end of a substantial amount of money. But what do you intend to do with this money?

The way you use the funds from the sale will vary, depending on your end goals for the business exit. As the vendor, this money can fund various different life goals for you, so it's crucial that you have a clear understanding of what you want to do with the sale proceeds.

Here are a few ways the funds could be used:

- **Build a nest egg for retirement** – if your goal is to retire, the price you sell the business for will need to provide enough funds to see you comfortably through your retirement. This means understanding your life goals, your outgoings and budgeting accordingly.

- **Form the capital for a new business idea** – you might be ready for a new business challenge. If so, your sale price needs to cover the startup costs needed to found a new business, while also covering your personal financial needs in the early stages.

- **Gift money to your family and the next generation** – it could be that you want to pass on your wealth to your family. If that's the case, you need to factor in the money you plan to gift, while also considering your own financial needs over the coming years.

- **Make donations to charities, social causes or political interests** – if you have particular charities and causes that are close to your heart, you may want to donate some of your sale proceeds to these institutions. Whatever you decide to donate, make sure that you're aware of the tax implications and how this affects your tax bill.

● **Invest the money to create a return** – you may want to invest the sale proceeds to create a healthy return and increase your wealth. This could mean investing in other startup projects, buying shares in growing companies or putting your money into a pension scheme or high-interest savings account. Again, knowing the tax implications of any kind of investment is vital if you're going to invest in a tax-efficient way.

Getting ready to exit the business

Selling your business is a big move, where it's invaluable to have the best possible support and advice to guide you through the sale process.

Talk to your accountant, tax agent and other business advisers and run your exit goals past them. As a founder, it can be difficult to be objective about your business. But external advisers have the advantage of being able to look from the outside in, with real objectivity. This helps you get independent, expert advice on your exit goals, your strategy and your tax planning.

◆◆◆

CHAPTER 31.
CREATING A PLAN FOR YOUR EXIT STRATEGY

Exiting your business is a big commitment. You're leaving behind everything you've built up, so it's vital that you have a plan of action and a clear route to your end goal. This means sitting down with your advisers to create a long-term exit strategy, with a plan that's aligned to your key goals, aims and financial commitments as the owner.

Coming up with this plan won't happen overnight. A business sale is a complex process with many different elements that all have to be considered. But by getting the basics down into a workable plan, you give yourself a helpful route map to guide you along the way.

Here are some of the fundamental things to think about when writing your plan.

Know your sale price

As the vendor, you need to come up with an asking price for the business. But this sale price isn't just driven by market forces. It's also dependent on how much money you need to raise.

If your aim is to start a new business, think about how much capital will be needed to get this idea off the ground. If your goal is to retire, you need to work out the size of the lump sum that will be needed. You could live for 20 or 30 years, post-retirement, so any cash raised has to provide you with your desired income and lifestyle for a number of years. And don't forget to allow for any tax that may be payable on profits you've made. Your accountant can help you estimate that.

Work out what funds you will need to retire or invest and make this total cost the benchmark for your ideal sale price. If you'd need £10M over 20 years, you know that your asking price must leave you with more than that after tax to provide a cushion for your finances.

Get the business valued

The next step is to understand the value of the business on the open market. This means talking to an M&A (mergers and acquisitions) expert, or working with the corporate finance team of your current accountancy provider.

Value is a complex measurement. It can be influenced by your brand's reputation, the business' current financial health, the worth of your company assets or the skill of your existing team. A change in any of these elements can have a huge impact on your sale value – and, as a result, the size of the profit that you and your departing shareholders will make from the sale.

If your current value is projected as £8M, but your initial asking price must be £10M or more, there's some work to do to add this value and boost your final sale price.

Decide on a successor

Every business needs a safe pair of hands at the top. Thinking about who will take over the reins, and how to make this transition run smoothly, is a vital part of your exit strategy.

A succession plan explains your own plans for retirement, who will take over your role and the timescales for this succession process. It may be that a family member is your intended successor. It could be that your intended buyer will take on the owner-manager role. Or it could be that a current member of your executive team is ready and willing to step into your shoes. Make sure you're clear about who the new boss will be, and how (and when) this person will succeed you as the leader of the business.

Work out the timescales for selling up

Selling your business is rarely something that happens quickly. Preparing for a sale can often begin years before the proposed date of exit, so it's important to be clear about your exit strategy and the key dates along the main timeline.

A five-year exit strategy is common, and you should allow at least two years to complete the process from beginning to end. Selling up may seem like the final scene in your business play, but in fact it's only the beginning of a long and protracted final act. The more you can do to plan each step of the exit, the more successful your final sale will be.

◆◆◆

CHAPTER 32. ADDING VALUE TO YOUR BUSINESS PRIOR TO AN EXIT

Generally speaking, an exit strategy will be put in place years before your planned exit date. This gives you time to work on your sale plan and deal with any succession issues. But more importantly, it gives you the time needed to add additional value to the business prior to a sale.

Every business has its own unique sale value, based on the size of the business, the worth of its assets and the perceived value of the company on the open market.

But what can you do to add value to your business and achieve a better sale price?

Make sure you're running a tight ship

When you sell a house, estate agents will advise you to redecorate, clear out the rubbish and add more to your sale price as a result. The same is true of selling a business.

A potential buyer will generally want to purchase a business that's in good shape. Sometimes a buyer will purchase a badly performing business to either a) whip it back into shape, or b) buy it cheap, sell off the assets and make a profit. However, if profit is what they're looking for, a well-organised and efficient business is a better prospect.

Adding value starts by doing your housekeeping and making sure the whole business is in a good position to hand over.

That means having:

● Modern, digital systems to keep your operations efficient, secure and well-integrated

● Excellent record-keeping, compliance and governance procedures in place

● A loyal customer base to provide stable sales and good revenues

● A good brand awareness and positive reputation in your sector

● Efficient executive, management, operational and administrative teams to run the business in the most smooth and effective ways.

Resolve any ongoing business issues

Every business will have a few ongoing business issues to contend with. These could include legal worries, court cases or bad debt in the business, and they can all have a negative impact on the company's value. The more you can do to resolve these issues and present a worry-free environment for the new owner, the better.

Work with your lawyers, solicitors, HR advisers and accountants to find resolutions for any long-standing problems in the business. If you can hand the business over without a long list of potential headaches for your buyer, that's likely to add value to the business. Trust is also important in a sale. Being transparent and open about any previous issues will also create a better relationship between you (the vendor) and your buyer.

Improve your financial health

Most buyers will be looking to purchase your business and turn a healthy profit. To do this, they'll want to know that the company is financially healthy. This means having books that balance and plenty of potential for them to continue this company as a profitable venture.

So, which areas of your finances should you be looking at? The key here is to be in control of your financial management, and to have a strategy in place that will improve each area of the business over time as you near your sale date.

This will include

- Strengthening your balance sheet, so you can present an attractive set of accounts

- Improving your profit and loss, by increasing revenues and cutting your expenses

- Boosting your cashflow position through careful cashflow management

- Reducing your debt liabilities, by resolving late payments and bad debts

- Polishing up your credit score, by partnering with a credit improvement specialist

- Making sure the business is well funded, by working closely with lenders.

Get your executive team ready to take over

You may well remain the lynchpin in your current business. But a business that's still 100% reliant on its founder is not an attractive proposition to a buyer. If the business is still reliant on your everyday operational input, and you then walk away, that business can no longer function effectively. To remedy this, you need to step back and get your team ready to take over.

The easiest way to do this, is to think about the key areas where you still have input, and to then systemise these and put them under the remit of a member of your executive team. If you're still signing off the payroll, pass this to your finance director. If you're still taking part in all client sales presentations, defer this to your sales director.

The key here is being able to sell up and step away from the business without there being any operational or leadership issues for the new owner.

Work with your advisers to proactively add value

Partnering with a mergers and acquisitions (M&A) specialist, or a corporate finance expert can do plenty to help you add value as part of your exit strategy and long-term plan.

Business advisers in the M&A market have the advantage of having worked on hundreds of different business sales, across a multitude of sectors. They know what looks attractive to a buyer and what the main red flags are in a purchase. And they know how important it is for your business to have a razor-sharp focus on adding value.

A good firm of advisers delivers a range of different advisory services. By gradually enhancing every element of the business, you'll end up with a far more attractive business to sell.

Keep any staff problems, legal issues or accounting challenges to a minimum, so the business is as attractive as possible to potential buyers, and the sale can be completed quickly.

Meeting your goals for the sale

To meet your personal and financial goals for this business sale, you want your company to be an attractive proposition on the open market. This process of added value isn't instantaneous, but with the right advice and planning, you can move towards a more valuable sale price.

◆◆◆

CHAPTER 33.
SELLING UP AND
MOVING ON: WHAT
HAPPENS NEXT?

Once you've sold your business and have received the funds from the sale, you're then faced with a big question: what happens next?

After years of guiding the course of this company, it will be tough to let go. But if the circumstances are right, and your motivation is true, there's no reason why exiting the business should be a sad occasion. You've built a stable business and personal legacy. You've employed a team of talented people and helped them drive their careers. And you've brought your products and/or services to a satisfied and loyal customer base.

So, how will you now focus your time and effort? Let's look at your options…

Retire and live out the entrepreneur's dream

If you're of a certain age, you may want to think about retiring. After many years of hard work, worries and stress, the thought of a business-free lifestyle may well be appealing. But retirement isn't for everyone. If you've thrived on the pressure, challenges and excitement of being the captain of your business ship, retiring may seem like a step away from the action.

On the flipside, the allure of a more relaxed lifestyle may be strong. With the proceeds from your sale, you should be in a position to make you, your family and those around you very comfortable. It may be that the entrepreneur's dream of building a business, selling up and retiring to a hot climate (with cocktails at the ready) is your idea of perfection.

Stay involved in the business

Even though you don't own the business anymore, it doesn't mean you have to step away completely from the company. You could remain involved in the business in some capacity, so you can 'keep your hand in' and support the future course of the business.

For example, you could become:

- **A joint partner in the business** – you may have only sold a part share in the business to your buyer and could be working as a joint partner with this new investor. This allows you to free up some capital, while maintaining an element of control and influence.

- **An external adviser or consultant** – you could advise the new owner and their board as an outside adviser. After all, who knows this business better than you? Becoming a consultant could well be an astute move and keeps you in the loop with the future path of the business – while charging out a consultancy fee as an added benefit.

- **A non-executive director (NED)** – you could join the board as a NED and use your years of personal experience to help guide and support the new owner and their board. If that's the route you choose, it's a good idea to retain some shares in the business, so you have a vested interest in the company's performance and your own share value.

- **An informal adviser to your family** – if you've handed the business down to the next generation of your family, they will almost certainly want your advice. You've been through the ups and downs of setting up the business, so you're in the best position to give your family the guidance and tips they need to run a smooth operation.

Set up a new business

With so much experience behind you, it could be that you're itching to start the whole business cycle again. If you've got the ideas, the capital and the motivation to start another new business, this can be a new and rewarding challenge to get your teeth into.

First time around, you'll have been a little green and less aware of the many pitfalls of founding a new business. With this experience now behind you, you're better prepared and more knowledgeable about what's required from a founder and business leader. We learn plenty from our mistakes, so you're in a great position to return to the business cycle again with a new idea.

As with any new businesses venture:

- Make sure you have a detailed breakdown of your business idea

- Write an in-depth business plan that maps out your journey

- Ensure you have the funding to get this idea off the ground

- Be prepared for a period of hard work and lower income before the company takes off

Do your bit for charity and your community

Doing something benevolent with your sale proceeds is a great path to explore. We all have interests and causes that are close to our heart, so supporting charities and community projects in these areas is a great way to use your money for long-term good.

Donating money to your chosen charity or social enterprise is also a triple whammy:

- You get to provide funding to causes that are close to your heart

- You can be philanthropic and help people who are in challenging situations

- You get the positive impact of tax breaks for donating to charity

You also have the option of putting your own time into working with these charitable causes. You can use your expertise and experience to guide them, help with fundraising or provide hands-on support at events, community projects or lobbying the Government for greater support.

The end of the road, or a new chapter?

Once the business is sold and you close your office door for the last time, you take a step into the unknown. But with so many varied and valuable options to choose from, your life post-exit need never be boring or predictable.

The potential is there for an exciting new venture, or the pleasure of relaxing in the sunshine by the pool. The choice, as they say, is yours and it's up to you to define the next chapter in your life and your business career.

◆◆◆

AFTERWORD

If you've enjoyed 'Help! I've Started A Business', please do drop me a line. You can contact me on Twitter @CommsBreakdown or on my website at commsbreakdown.com/contact

If you bought the book through Amazon, I'd greatly appreciate it if you could leave a review. Tell me how it was to read, what helped you out and how the book compares to other business titles you've read along your business journey.

amazon.com/Steve-Ash/e/B07WLQ2K6L

ACKNOWLEDGEMENTS

Thanks to the team at BOMA Marketing for inspiring me to write the original content for this book. If you're an accountant, sign up with BOMA to access awesome pre-written business content to share with your clients. Check them out at bomamarketing.com

Many thanks also to all the accountants I've worked with over the years. It's the many hours of phone calls, interviews and ghost blog-writing that have expanded my business knowledge to a point where I could actually write this book!

Thanks also to the 2014 team at Xero UK for inspiring me to learn more about the startup and small business journey in the first place. They're at xero.com

Finally, thanks to my family for supporting me in my writing endeavours. All those cups of decaff coffee and chocolate biscuits did not go to waste!

◆◆◆

ABOUT THE AUTHOR

Steve Ash

Steve is an experienced content writer. He's worked in marketing for PwC, as a content writer for Xero cloud accounting software and as a digital content manager for The Profitable Firm.

He now runs CommsBreakdown, a content writing business, providing bespoke content, branding and digital marketing concepts to a cross-section of tech startups, fintech companies, established businesses and accounting firms.

Steve grew up in Hertfordshire in the UK, but now lives in Australia with his partner, Joanna, and their young daughter. When he's not writing, he'll be found playing guitar, making bad techno and attempting to ration his chocolate intake.

Contact Steve on Twitter @CommsBreakdown
Visit his website at www.commsbreakdown.com

BOOKS BY THIS AUTHOR

How To Write Killer Content For Your Startup

Want to create killer content for your startup? This book is a one-stop shop for polishing your writing skills, learning about digital marketing and creating the killer content you need to kickstart your business.

Each chapter gives you simple, easy-to-follow tips, with advice on how to write: website content, blog posts, email campaigns, social media content and content plans.

Going Freelance: Building Work Around Your Life

Going Freelance is your 101 guide to freelancing and starting a self-employed business.

Learn how to get your freelance business off the ground. Find your first paying customers and make a living from your freelance skills. And get the lowdown on how to manage your workload, maximise your time and improve your work/life balance.

Printed in Great Britain
by Amazon